# Poor Girl, Rich Life
### DISCOVER HIS PLAN TO PROSPER YOU

### Romona Robinson

*Jesus looked at them and said, "With man this is impossible, but with God all things are possible."*
—Matthew 19:26 NIV

*Poor Girl, Rich Life*
Trilogy Christian Publishers A Wholly Owned Subsidiary of Trinity Broadcasting Network
2442 Michelle Drive Tustin, CA 92780
Copyright © 2023 by Romona Robinson
Scripture quotations marked EHV are taken from The Holy Bible, Evangelical Heritage Version®, EHV®, © 2019 Wartburg Project, Inc. All rights reserved. Scripture quotations marked ESV are taken from the ESV® Bible (The Holy Bible, English Standard Version®), copyright © 2001 by Crossway Bibles, a publishing ministry of Good News Publishers. ©All rights reserved. Scripture quotations marked MSG are taken from *THE MESSAGE*, copyright © 1993, 2002, 2018 by Eugene H. Peterson. Used by permission of NavPress. All rights reserved. Represented by Tyndale House Publishers, Inc. Scripture quotations marked NASB are taken from the New American Standard Bible® (NASB), Copyright © 1960, 1962, 1963, 1968, 1971, 1972, 1973, 1975, 1977, 1995 by The Lockman Foundation. Used by permission. www.Lockman.org. Scripture quotations marked NIV are taken from the Holy Bible, New International Version®, NIV®. Copyright © 1973, 1978, 1984, 2011 by Biblica, Inc.™ Used by permission of Zondervan. All rights reserved worldwide. www.zondervan.com. The "NIV" and "New International Version" are trademarks registered in the United States Patent and Trademark Office by Biblica, Inc.™ Scripture quotations marked TLB are taken from The Living Bible copyright © 1971. Used by permission of Tyndale House Publishers, a Division of Tyndale House Ministries, Carol Stream, Illinois 60188. All rights reserved. Scripture quotations marked KJV are taken from the King James Version of the Bible. Public domain.
No part of this book may be reproduced, stored in a retrieval system, or transmitted by any means without written permission from the author. All rights reserved. Printed in the USA.
Rights Department, 2442 Michelle Drive, Tustin, CA 92780.
Trilogy Christian Publishing/TBN and colophon are trademarks of Trinity Broadcasting Network.
For information about special discounts for bulk purchases, please contact Trilogy Christian Publishing.
Trilogy Disclaimer: The views and content expressed in this book are those of the author and may not necessarily reflect the views and doctrine of Trilogy Christian Publishing or the Trinity Broadcasting Network.
Manufactured in the United States of America
10 9 8 7 6 5 4 3 2 1
Library of Congress Cataloging-in-Publication Data is available.
ISBN: 979-8-88738-663-8
E-ISBN: 979-8-88738-664-5
*Poor Girl, Rich Girl* is a work of nonfiction. Some names and identifying details have been changed.

**Part of the proceeds of this book will be donated to organizations that serve the needs of children.**

# DEDICATION

To my late mom, my ten siblings, and the families of Wilson City, Missouri, who watched over me and protected me as I grew into a healthy and confident adult. This book is dedicated to each of you.

# CONTENTS

Introduction................................... 9

   Chapter 1: Know Your Worth.................... 15

**Part 1: Heal from Money Trauma.................. 33**

   Chapter 2: Uncover Your Why................... 35

   Chapter 3: You Don't Know
   What You Don't Know.......................... 55

   Chapter 4: The Gift That Keeps on Giving ......... 71

**Part 2: Reset Your Money Mindset................. 83**

   Chapter 5: The Poor, the Rich,
   and What's Possible .......................... 85

   Chapter 6: Hoarding Money
   and Reckless Spending........................ 109

   Chapter 7: Excess Does Not Equal Success........ 121

   Chapter 8: Friends and Financial Foolishness ...... 147

   Chapter 9: Start Expecting the Unexpected ........ 163

   Chapter 10: Show Me the Money................. 173

   Chapter 11: Protect What You Earn .............. 183

Chapter 12: Chasing Money Instead of Living . . . . . 197

Chapter 13: The Power to Say No . . . . . . . . . . . . . . 207

**Part 3: The Payoff? . . . . . . . . . . . . . . . . . . . . . . . . . . . 217**

Chapter 14: To Whom Much Is Given . . . . . . . . . . . . 219

Chapter 15: Financial Freedom . . . . . . . . . . . . . . . . . 229

Chapter 16: The Inheritance . . . . . . . . . . . . . . . . . . . 237

Chapter 17: My True Worth . . . . . . . . . . . . . . . . . . . 247

Epilogue . . . . . . . . . . . . . . . . . . . . . . . . . . . . . . . . . . . 265

Acknowledgments . . . . . . . . . . . . . . . . . . . . . . . . . . . . 271

About Romona . . . . . . . . . . . . . . . . . . . . . . . . . . . . . 273

# INTRODUCTION

I will never forget my twenty-seventh birthday.

I was dead broke. No job, about to be kicked out of my apartment, surviving on 92 cents for dinner each night eating ramen noodles, with credit collectors calling and demanding money. Just months prior, I had been a successful television anchor and reporter working in South Carolina. I couldn't believe how quickly things had changed.

Have you ever faced an unexpected, life-altering financial crisis? If so, you'll probably recognize the deep fear that washed over me that evening, a rush of emotion taking control of my body as I contemplated my next steps.

As I lay face-planted on my bed, sobbing, asking God "Why me?" thoughts of being a poor six-year-old girl growing up in a rural, dirt-road community tucked away in Missouri's heartland came into view.

They were painful memories of my single mom suffering chronic exhaustion as a shoe seamstress. She worked a miracle raising her kids (eleven of us!) on just $2 an hour, and she still managed to save.

It was one of the biggest money lessons my mom drilled into my head as a child: "Save ya money, 'cause ya never know when hard times will hit."

Fast-forward two decades, and there I was, a single, college-educated, corporate girl who made mountains more money than my mom, but I hadn't managed it well.

As my tears dried, I continued to ask myself: *Why am I in this predicament? How could I have left myself so vulnerable, with no safety net? I'd been raised better. Shouldn't I have done better?*

What I didn't know at the time, and wouldn't come to know until decades later, is that my money struggles were rooted in something much deeper than careless spending habits or the lack of a savings account. It wasn't until I began the research for this book that I uncovered the concept of financial trauma. A relatively new area of study, it seeks to help us to recognize that although experiences we have growing up may seem unrelated to our money problems, they may actually form our later financial habits on a subconscious level.

As I dove into the research, I learned why I had allowed myself to become broke and why, even after bouncing back from that setback, I would go on to make more money mistakes. Having grown up in poverty, I was still carrying around childhood wounds of scarcity, insecurity, and inferiority because of what I didn't have. I didn't like being teased as a "poor girl," the one who wore jeans that were too short or shoes that had holes in them. Spending carelessly as an adult was my way of trying to make up for things I'd never had as a child—fashionable clothes, fancy house parties, or pricey vacations. I felt important

## Introduction

when I bought stuff, even things I didn't need or really even want. *I found validation and worthiness in the things I purchased.*

Does this sound familiar to you? Discovering my WHY was one of the first steps toward my money success. Maybe your early money story is different. Maybe you lived through your parents' divorce and watched your family's finances drastically change. Maybe you were a trust-fund baby, a child who never went without—until your dad lost his job. Perhaps you or your parents were caught up in the 2008 housing crisis, and your home was foreclosed on. Maybe, like me, you were shunned by some of your peers, seen as an outcast because of your zip code. Whatever your money trauma, chances are, those events shaped your relationship with your money and how you spend it, either inadvertently or consciously.

If you've picked up this book, I'm guessing you're struggling with your finances today, and looking for advice on how to move from scarcity to financial freedom. I want to help you on that path. Although I was raised in poverty, I've managed to plow a path from the bottom 99 percent of this country to the top of my career—and I believe you can reach your financial goals—whatever they might be. But here's the thing: This is not a book filled with financial strategies, charts, and figures asking you to give up your daily Starbucks and become frugal. There are hundreds of books on the market that provide those tools. Instead *Poor Girl, Rich Life* is about what

I've learned over a long career—and the life I've lived with and without. A life that involved careless spending habits and poor money choices and the meaning behind it. And I believe that by uncovering your money trauma and identifying the triggers that derail your financial goals, you can rid yourself of old lies, reset your money mindset, and get on the path to true prosperity and wealth.

Now, I am not a therapist or a financial guru, but I do know people. As an Emmy award–winning journalist, speaker, author, and philanthropist, I have spent more than thirty years interviewing thousands of people about their lives and their issues, and I've gained a keen sense of what keeps them up at night. Pocketbook issues are always top of mind. I understand the challenges you're facing—and I've been there myself. I'll use both my story and the stories of others to help you reconsider your own relationship with money and empower you to move forward with more wisdom and bravery as you work toward financial security.

Perhaps most importantly, this book places the pursuit of wealth within the context of God's abundance. True wealth comes from understanding our value and worth in His eyes; and financial freedom means being a good steward of God's blessings. My knowledge of money and faith comes from decades of growing both. I've gone from a childhood of hopelessness, through the embarrassment of financial failure, to a worry-free financial life. I didn't get here until I started to have a healthy relationship with

## Introduction

money and believe in God's promises about wealth. These promises became the key to how I would acquire money, spend it, save it, and share it.

I started writing this book several months before the pandemic began in 2020, and the economic tailspin in which the virus threw us affirmed why I must share my story. My hope is that it will empower and motivate people to take ownership of their money and start saving more.

No matter what your walk is in life, this book can motivate you to reimagine your financial future, drop the pretense, and change your money attitude. You may be part of the 78 percent of Americans who are living paycheck to paycheck, tired of watching your bank account drain and your credit card balances rise, wondering where the money is going. This book is also for the high-income earner playing rich—with little net worth. For the woman not being paid her worth—afraid to fight for equity, which is crucial to ensuring a nice nest egg. For the faith-filled person who is grinding away every day, believing in God's promises, yet screaming out, as I did, "Where is my blessing? Where is the prosperity, hope and good future You promised?"

This book will serve as a roadmap to what is possible in your finances when you are willing to do the head work and the heart work required to address the way you want to authentically show up in the world. It is divided into three parts to guide you through the financial lessons necessary to learn to live a life of financial security. Part 1 focuses on rooting out the financial baggage we all bring to the table. We'll uncover the money trauma of which you may be unaware, and we'll discuss the learned behaviors we subconsciously allow to dictate how we handle our money. Part 2 is all about the mindset switch. Once you pinpoint what triggers push you to overspend—or why you allow society to dictate what you wear, the car you drive, or the house you buy—then you can flip that switch and begin to take practical steps to work toward a life of financial freedom. Finally, Part 3 showcases the lasting impact of making informed financial choices God's way. We'll consider how God holds us responsible for what we've been blessed with—and not just our money. He wants us to use our talents, our knowledge, and our time not just to enrich ourselves, but to benefit others. Ultimately, true richness is found in the people you touch and the lasting connections you make through serving God with what He's given you.

It is my hope that you will conclude, as I did, that by letting go of past traumas, looking fear straight in the eye, and gaining godly wisdom about money, you can overcome your money issues. Are you ready to get started?

## CHAPTER 1
# KNOW YOUR WORTH

*You must find the courage to leave the table if respect is no longer being served.*
—**Tene Edwards**

It was a half hour before news time. Like any other day, I was in the dressing room frantically painting on "my face" to make the deadline. As I leaned into the mirror, making sure there was enough blush, eyeliner, and powder to withstand the harsh studio lights, I heard the *click-clack* of someone in high heels walking down the tile hallway. It was a confident walk, that of a woman who had mastered the art of striding professionally in pumps. In a moment, her reflection appeared in the mirror. It was one of my on-air colleagues.

I said hello, looking at her through the mirror, then continued to apply makeup as we made small talk.

Soon she shifted the conversation. "Romona, I've always wanted to thank you for what you did for me and other anchorwomen in this city," she whispered, still standing behind me but visible in the mirror.

I did a slow one-eighty turn to face her, stunned. "What do you mean? Thank me for what?"

A deep furrow formed on her brow as she sensed my body tense, but she persisted. "For standing up and demanding equal pay. It opened doors for all of us."

Tilting my head, my lips parted, and I grew quiet, frozen in shock. It's a natural response when someone starts to talk about your money—you clam up and shut down. I waited for my puzzled mind to catch up and direct me toward an appropriate response. I thought, *What can she possibly know about me and my salary, how much it is, and what exactly I do?* An anchor's salary is highly confidential.

"Thank you," I mustered. The comment blindsided me. I was stunned anyone knew what I had accomplished more than a decade earlier. Reliving what I had pulled off in 1999 still sends shivers up my spine.

## All They Can Say Is No

"Why can't I get paid what male anchors across the street are making?" I pressed my television attorney. I was huddled with my high-powered rep at a swanky Cleveland restaurant as he delivered the discouraging news that my station would never pay the raise for which I had been asking.

*Chapter 1: Know Your Worth*

I was not giving up. I grilled him further. "This isn't fair."

"That's just how it is, Romona. It's how it's always been. Men are the kings in this market, and they get paid accordingly," he explained.

"That doesn't make it right," I shot back.

I was the primary evening anchor at *Channel 3 News*. After over a decade in Cleveland, I reportedly had the highest Q-rating among news talent—the score that measures a talent's familiarity and popularity in their community. Upon my arrival at WKYC-TV in 1997, the station had ranked number three, sometimes fourth, in the market. But within a few short years of my tenure, the ratings soared. My partner, Tim White, joined the team in 1999, and we later enjoyed the number-one eleven o'clock newscast in the city.

"I know one person is not responsible for a winning newscast. We have a great product; it's a team effort. But if the ratings jump exponentially when you're hired, that's telling," I argued to my lawyer.

I had worked hard for those ratings. As a leading anchor, I was up early, fielding calls from my news director about assignments. At times producers would ask me to use my trustworthiness and likability to call politicians and controversial figures and help garner tough-to-get interviews for the station. Hours before my shift began, I'd scour local and a few national papers and sometimes listen to talk radio, all to prepare for my newscast. I have never been one of those anchors who could or would just "wing it" on the air. I wanted an in-depth understanding of what I was reporting or whom I was interviewing. I also liked to offer story ideas about our daily coverage in afternoon editorial meetings.

In other words, I invested myself in the work, beyond the job description. From my early days as a producer and street reporter in Charleston, South Carolina, I knew the importance of forging good relationships with sources within the police department, with top city leaders, and with other important players in the community. I anchored presidential election specials, moderated local debates, and interviewed legislators and heads of state.

I served my city. I spoke, hosted charitable events, and coproduced a weekly *Romona's Kids* segment, which I started in 1990 at WUAB-TV in Cleveland to motivate our city's youth to greater achievements. I even told children they could write to me if they needed extra guidance. I spent a lot of time writing back to mostly tweens and teens. I was bent on changing lives, one letter at a time.

I loved my work, but the pace and workload could be exhausting, not to mention the demands on a female anchor to always look flawless—often requiring a makeup artist and a hair and clothes stylist. The pressure to stay fit and youthful looking was enormous. I could outwork anyone—and I often did. But I also believed I should be compensated for it.

## Chapter 1: Know Your Worth

For two weeks I had pressured my attorney to seek a salary on par with what the male news giants across town made.

He'd again push back, saying I'd never get it. "Let's just ask for a few thousand more than what they're offering. It's still a lot of money. Anyone would jump at that offer," he continued.

"But it's much less than the men make, and my Q numbers are higher than theirs. I've worked hard for this, and I deserve it. I have one of the highest-rated newscasts in its time slot in Cleveland right now. I should even make more," I pressed.

"Trust me, it's not going to happen," he said. My persistence agitated him.

"We have to ask. All they can say is no." I waited for him to agree. Quite frankly, I didn't care if it hadn't been done before.

In that awkward silence, I realized I was starting to come into my own, finding my voice and my worth.

As a child, I had been shy, an introvert; speaking up about anything was not part of my makeup. I was always afraid to push the envelope. But now, after years of being battle-tested in my field by sexual harassment, sexism, racism, wrongful termination, and a host of other challenges women face every day in the workplace, I was self-assured, confident in my abilities, and determined to get what I was worth.

"I can ask, but you'll never get it, Romona," the attorney said, looking at me in frustration. "I suggest you get your head out of the clouds and back down here on earth, where the rest of us live. Remember, you have responsibilities, and they come due every month."

I didn't need him to remind me of that. Even though I was single, I was helping my younger sisters with their college tuition. I was worried about having enough to protect my mom; I wanted to buy her a home in a safer neighborhood after drugs had moved into the neighborhood where she lived. I was helping a friend pay private tuition for her two kids to escape a dangerous public school in her neighborhood. I was giving to my church and the charities I loved.

I resented that I needed to explain to my attorney what I brought to the table. I started to ask myself if he was truly working in my best interest.

While my attorney had served me well, I was no longer willing to play the role of a dutiful client who allowed him to speak for me. I had grown into a strong adult, who was willing to look fear in the eye. I could speak for myself.

More than that, I began to see that legal smarts were no match for God's grace.

My next move was probably the boldest and most frightening. My contract with my lawyer was expiring, and I decided to not re-sign with his firm. Instead, I would take a leap of faith, represent myself, and negotiate my

*Chapter 1: Know Your Worth*

own work contract.

## An Asset to the Company

His beady, expressionless eyes looked like he was still alive, staring straight at me from the plate: the two-pound lobster with garlic mashed potatoes the waiter had just brought and placed on the table in front of me.

My general manager marveled at the mammoth crustacean I was about to devour.

"You know, it's my favorite, and I've never been shy about eating." We both laughed.

My GM was treating me to dinner at a fancy downtown Cleveland restaurant after my six o'clock newscast. We were seated in the back—a spot for a private conversation.

It was a meeting to talk about a new deal. I wanted money on par with what the male anchors in my city made. My boss was a tall, imposing figure, even more so in the large, padded shoulders of his business suit. He hung his jacket on a nearby coatrack, a sign he was getting comfortable for an uncomfortable chat.

The food was perfect; the dialogue, not so much.

He had a reputation for being frighteningly firm when it came to negotiations. It was easy to see why. He took his time speaking, carefully crafting his words, sometimes prolonging them as he gathered his thoughts. His massive arms interlocked, with one hand caressing his chin at times, his eyes canvassing the restaurant and then the ceiling before slowing making their way back down to me. It was his signature style, which gave you a few seconds to gather your thoughts and contemplate your next move.

He was a seasoned pro in the business and had accomplished a great deal since arriving at Channel 3 a year after I had. Under his leadership, we became the first local station in digital broadcasting.

"You have been an asset to the company, Romona. Corporate is pleased with what we've been able to accomplish in Cleveland, and you're a huge part of that. The new contract I presented to you is fair." He took out a pen and scribbled something on a yellow Post-it Note. He slid the small piece of paper across the dinner table toward me.

I was trying to keep a straight face, not showing emotion, hoping my elevated blood pressure was not visible, but inside I was praying for a number close to what I'd asked for.

I slowly lifted the note and read it. After taking several deep breaths, I responded. "This is a good start," I said. "I appreciate your interest in continuing what we've built. But this is nowhere near what my male peers across the street make. May I?" I motioned, asking to borrow his pen. Flipping the Post-it Note over, I scrawled a different number. "I was thinking of something in this ballpark. It's more in line with what I should be paid."

*Chapter 1: Know Your Worth*

His face was now devoid of warmth. "How could you possibly know what those other anchors make?" he inquired.

"Any attorney worth their salt can discover a ballpark figure," I shot back. "You know they talk."

"I'd be careful listening to people throwing out erroneous, inflated numbers to you," he warned.

"I've done my homework. I know that in the nation's top-twenty television markets, the number I gave you is the going rate for primary male anchors. Your number is far too low."

There was still a year left on my current deal, so I felt I had plenty of time to keep negotiating. I also knew that when a station negotiates a year out, it signals they want to keep you. If they wait until the last minute, it's to stress you out, hoping you'll take less money for fear of losing your job.

"It's getting late, and you have a show to do," my GM said. "Let's table this and talk again in a few days."

## No One Could Sell Me Like I Could

Back at the station, I stewed in my office, going over and over how I needed to advocate for myself and stick to my guns. It was crucial I felt confident when asking to be paid for the value I brought to the station. Plus, I knew if I was going to have a shot at prosperity and fulfilling my dreams, I had to stop settling for cheap. That money was going to be my security blanket someday.

My childhood crept into my mind—not the good stuff, not the encouraging words of Mom's wisdom and my faith, which says that God wants to "give you the desires of your heart" (Ps. 37:4 NIV). Instead, I allowed negativity to rule my mind. I thought of being out of work, not being able to pay my bills. Maybe I wouldn't be able to find another job right away.

If you're like me, you've probably been here before—in a situation where you know you aren't being valued as you should, and you start to doubt yourself. As it got closer to airtime, however, my mood switched to a more courageous one, and I realized I could either tap into the negative thoughts or turn my uncertainty into strength.

I was doing the work, building my name and my value. Romona Robinson had become a household name in northeast Ohio. I had a stellar reputation in the community, synonymous with integrity, respect, and class.

Should I just shut up, be thankful I had a job, and not upset the apple cart? That wasn't the woman Mom had raised.

I was not willing to work harder and for less than a man.

On average, women are sorely underpaid, earning about 77 cents to every dollar a man makes while doing the same work. For black women, it's only 62 cents.

## Chapter 1: Know Your Worth

In my conversations with women in my industry and elsewhere, each of them knew they deserved more, but some were afraid to ask for it. Those brave enough to ask got a little more at times, but many were threatened with termination—which immediately shut down the conversation.

I would soon discover, no one could sell me like I could.

When you grow up in poverty as I did, you might believe you don't deserve a lot more. But you do—even when others say it's impossible.

I guess I hoped my boss would naturally see my hard work and reward me accordingly. But when I realized that wasn't going to happen, I knew I could not be passive. Ever since my television career began, back in 1983, I had been afraid to ask for more money, not wanting to appear greedy or ungrateful—or worse, get fired. The fear of losing my salary always outweighed my gut, which said I had earned a raise.

But now, taking the risk to negotiate my own lucrative contract had become imperative. My self-confidence had grown, and so had my wisdom. I wasn't just praying more; I was praying boldly, and I mentally worked on my belief that God would see me through.

Years of reading and believing the Word also matured my faith to stand up to fear. I had to believe the words of Hebrews 13:6: "The Lord is my Helper, and I am not afraid of anything that mere man can do to me" (TLB).

During my negotiations, like many of you have probably done, I leaned into my faith and the promises in God's Word for times of trouble. I could hear Mom's voice hammering into my head as a child, telling me to stop being afraid, to stand up and fight for myself.

I loved my work, but I didn't think I could work for a station that didn't recognize my worth and want to pay me for it.

## "There Are Thousands of Romonas Out There"

Tiny hairs still rise on the back of my neck as I recall the back-and-forth negotiations that went on for those several weeks. Management tried the tried-and-true "good cop/bad cop" technique—the GM was the heavy while my news director played nice, speaking to me privately to gauge my head space.

Then came the hard press. I was summoned to my general manager's office, and the heat was on.

As I entered the room, there was an unusual silence. The GM kept looking at a stack of papers on his desk. My eyes wandered around his impressive office. Modern, chic chairs done up in beechwood and metal flanked his massive desk, behind which he sat in his large leather chair. The wall of floor-to-ceiling windows in his corner office provided a spectacular view of sunlight shimmering

## Chapter 1: Know Your Worth

atop crashing waves on the lake.

"Come on in and have a seat," he instructed, still engrossed in his work. He slowly lifted his head to make eye contact.

His facial expression was like a blank sheet of paper. He rose from his chair to grab his business jacket off the corner coatrack—it completed his usual corporate attire, consisting of a crisp white shirt and khaki slacks. He slumped back in his seat, brows creased and face tense.

"Romona, I've talked with corporate, and the money you're asking for is not doable. We just can't justify spending that kind of money." He paused. "You are fantastic in the community, great at your job, and we're happy with your work here, but your request is more than we're willing to spend."

He pulled another yellow Post-it Note off the pad, wrote a number on it, and slid it across his desk. "Take a look at this number. That's what we're willing to offer you in a new, three-year deal."

It was a slightly larger amount than before, but still well below what I knew I should be making. Before I could respond, he continued. "There are thousands of Romonas out there, waiting to take your job. I have their résumés right here in my files."

"And I know there are probably other GMs in town who would love to have Romona join their staff," was my bold, quick-witted comeback.

The scowl on his face was evidence the verbal punch had landed.

Still, I had become as stiff as a mannequin, hardened by his words. I painted on a happy face, not revealing my fear of being replaced. A battle was raging in my head between the anxiety that sneaked up on me quietly and my faith that God would prevail.

A few days later, I was called back to his office. He looked especially confident perched in his massive seat, exuding power and prestige. I don't remember his exact words, but he closed his speech with words that tumbled slowly and cautiously out of his mouth. "We're going to move on if you don't accept this offer." His eyes were laser-focused on me.

Every scenario quickly played in my head. Over and over, I heard the words: "You're gonna be fired. You're gonna be fired."

I tried to close my mind to his angry, gravelly low voice. My body tensed, and my throat felt dry. I swallowed, and again shot him a calm, friendly look, even though a storm raged inside me. All my hard work, all the time I had put into my craft, everything I had done at the station and in the community—none of it seemed to matter to the company. We were winning in the ratings, and we were rewarded with lavish, catered prime rib and champagne dinners because of it. The decadence inside our new thirty-two-million-dollar, state-of-the-art television station was incredible, including the art on the walls, an

*Chapter 1: Know Your Worth*

upper floor the public could rent for events, a gift shop, an exercise facility, a comfortable cafeteria, and of course, the backdrop: Lake Erie itself.

With all our success, it felt like they were printing money, but none of it was trickling down to me.

I had to ask myself if I was ready to turn my back on everything I had built and walk away or if I should just accept the status quo. The offer my GM made that day was another lowball offer that didn't come close to what was fair.

## Know Your Worth

While there are many factors that contribute to money struggles—all of which we'll dive into in the coming chapters—it all starts with knowing your worth. No matter your income, financial success is always tied to your ability to increase your earning power—whatever that number is for you. When we are rooted in the security of who God made us to be, we can approach money out of a place of abundance rather than fear.

I start with this story because it was a tipping point in my career, one in which I found the grit and bravery needed to embark on the road to true prosperity. During this time, I truly found my voice. I felt a mental shift taking place, a call to finally be strong and believe in what I had to offer. Asking for a raise is one of the single most important things a woman—or anyone—can do to increase their earning power over the course of their career. It's vital to build wealth during your prime earning years. But for many women, the ask isn't easy.

Maybe you've convinced yourself that you don't deserve a raise—that you're not as good as the guy in the next cubicle because of where you come from or where you went to school. Maybe you're afraid of negative ramifications or even unemployment, especially if you are the head of a household.

I've learned that fear can sometimes mask itself as a safety net. Fear tells us what we can't do, what not to do, what raise we'll never get. Sometimes hearing "no" prevents us from being assertive and receiving what we've earned. But I knew I needed to put on my "big girl pants" and speak up for myself.

I was simply asking to be compensated for what I brought to the table. Yet in return, I heard the words, "The station will move on with someone else." I decided to use what God gave me—a firm, yet emotional approach, stressing my attachment to my work, my colleagues, and the health of the station. If I were going to accept his lowball offer, now would be the time. I was at a point in my life that I had learned to live bravely when it came to asking for my worth.

"I'm sorry to hear that," I finally told my GM. "I have had the time of my life representing this station. Thank you." Abruptly, without giving him an answer, I stood to walk out without uttering another word, hoping he hadn't

## Chapter 1: Know Your Worth

detected the tears forming behind my eyes.

*

My resolve and strength that day triggered deep memories from my past. You've been reading about the strong, confident, self-assured woman I am today. But how did I get here? Where did this mental courage I now possessed come from? Where did I come up with the belief that I deserved to be prosperous if I did the work? Where did I find the power to stand my ground and not be taken advantage of?

I'll get to all those questions, and you'll find out how these negotiations eventually ended. First, though, I've got to go back to the beginning—both yours and mine. To develop a mindset of wealth that can lead to financial freedom, I must start by uncovering my "whys" and the ways my early experiences shaped the way I approach money today.

PART 1

# HEAL FROM MONEY TRAUMA

# CHAPTER 2
# UNCOVER YOUR WHY

A detail of United States Secret Service team members appear to be all around me. Their eyes are resting squarely on my hands.

I'm nervously threading my microphone up and underneath my black top and royal blue blazer. Their hawkish stares are making me uncomfortable, but their stance is understandable given the circumstances.

It's April 2011, and I'm seated in the Diplomatic Room inside the White House. It is one of three oval rooms that serve as the primary entrance for the First Family. Seated directly in front of me and looking straight into my eyes as I continue to fumble with my mic is the most powerful man in the free world. I have garnered a rare, exclusive, sit-down interview with the current president of the United States, Barack Obama.

I can feel my heart racing. It is seemingly beating twice its normal rate, because that darn tethered microphone, which is usually attached inconspicuously for me under my wardrobe on a remote shoot, is my responsibility at the White House. The wrestling match I am having with this one-inch mouthpiece and wire requires a lot of maneuvering as I try to pin it to my lapel beneath my top and keep the wiring out of the camera's view. It slips out of my hand and slithers back down toward my belly, and I do a deep dive for the clip—right in view of the president. Really, though, there was nowhere to escape, for privacy. The president was patiently seated, already mic'ed up, powdered and plumped by hordes of staffers. As I struggled, I desperately wished for a wireless mic. As it has no cords, you simply clip it on your jacket and you're ready to go.

My exterior wore a soft expression, but inside, my brain had exploded with panic. Keep in mind this was only a matter of ten seconds, but to me it felt like sixty!

Being the gentlemen that he was and sensing my discomfort, the president immediately spoke words to break the awkward moment as I recovered. Smiling warmly, he asked, "Now, where are you from, Romona? Tell me about your people . . ."

His question flooded me with memories of my childhood. Being in the presence of the president of the United States, in the most famous "white house" in the world, I couldn't help but recognize how my story had changed and grown, both professionally and financially. I was reminded of how this moment felt like the fulfillment

## Chapter 2: Uncover Your Why

of prophecy. I had sat next to my mom in our own tiny "white house" in Missouri decades ago and dreamt of this very moment.

Take this journey with me as we begin to delve into the things that have shaped us and possibly hindered our money habits. Let's think back to where our stories began.

## What Shapes Us

When I think back to the landscape of scarcity and constant financial hardship I experienced in my childhood town, it fills me with both joy and sorrow. My hometown was a place of significant struggle and poverty, but it was also the place where my future was foretold, although in those years, I couldn't see the award-winning journalist I would become.

Wilson City, Missouri, is a tiny hamlet of ten segregated villages created in the 1940s to house sharecroppers who had been evicted from rented homes owned by whites. It was known as the "forgotten town" because outsiders never visited unless a midwife was called to deliver a baby, or unless someone needed house repairs. Even the school bus didn't venture too far into our town; we walked out to the edge of town for pickup.

Our town was so tiny it was hardly a speck on the map, hidden deep in the bowels of Missouri's bootheel. It had a single dirt road of constant, endless hardship for 212 people—twelve of them being my family members. There were about sixty homes, a general store, and a rusted-out playground with tattered swings, bent monkey bars, and a seesaw minus the seats. I can still hear the joyful screams of my siblings and me as we played, thankful for even a junkyard playground.

My people were God-fearing, deeply rooted in their religion. They were mostly destitute farm laborers, with not much education, but they were full of faith. For their ancestors, working took precedence over an education, and our community seemed to adopt that family tradition. Wilson City is a place where people took pride in honest work—even if that work didn't pay enough even to live on. Most folks earned somewhere way south of five grand a year in the mid-1960s.

Wilson City is where kids like me suffered a grim future. If you were lucky, you would graduate from high school, marry a local boy who could take care of you, and produce babies young. Some who were not so lucky dropped out of school, picked up odd jobs, and faced a bleak future. Then there were the dreamers, like me—the ones determined to defy the statistics and find a better way. We dreamers envisioned living the American Dream, including a higher education, a viable career, and ultimately, home ownership.

Some of the hardest-working people you'll ever meet live in my rural hometown. The blinding bright sun would reveal a silhouette of a neighbor across the way perched on his tractor in his worn overalls, continually wiping

## Chapter 2: Uncover Your Why

sweat off his forehead as he plowed his soybean field. They were also the most generous folks. They'd rescue a stranger's pickup stuck in a muddy ditch without pause—the risk of being soaked in the brown stuff, not a problem. They'd help to feed your kids when you lost your job. They'd rush to aid a senior lady slowly walking down the dusty dirt road clutching her purse and groceries, hoping malnourished stray dogs didn't snatch her purchases (they're meaner than hungry lions).

I vividly remember the voices of men who'd gone catfishing as they drove along our milelong trail in their rickety pickups yelling, "Catfish here." If Mom had extra, she'd plunk down a few bucks for four or five of the tasty, tangy bottom-feeders. I'd have to go out back, find a stray wooden board, grab the sharpest butcher knife Momma had, and chop their heads off. The smell alone when it came time to scale them was repulsive. And I remember more smells: the rabbit, squirrel, and possum hunters who would knock at our door with their prized possessions thrown over their shoulders, the lifeless carcasses, some of their remains dripping onto our concrete front steps, the heads still intact. Mom would only purchase the ones already skinned, decapitated, dissected, declawed, and cleaned.

Most of the houses in our town were white and gray wood-planked, some on stilts, some in disrepair. Shacks rotted away that should have been condemned long ago. Old furniture, appliances, and anything else abandoned were strewn in the front and back yards—overgrown weeds shielding some of them. The trunks of mature trees split in half were left leaning to fend for themselves, no doubt the victims of a severe storm or two.

While many of the homes were old and in disrepair, ours was one of the newest. In 1965, Mom bought an empty lot for $170 and made a $250 down payment on our newly built $7,500 little white house, courtesy of a low-income FHA loan. Mom possessed the unrelenting spirit of always trying to get ahead. I watched her scrape, claw, and save to afford her piece of the American Dream. Our 1,100-square-foot, four-bedroom-and-one-bath home at the end of a dirt road was surrounded by miles of soybean fields, cornfields, and wildflowers that would burst into a colorful maze of heaven on earth.

Trying to save for a home and feed her children on $1.25 an hour in 1965 might have seemed impossible to most, but Mom found work wherever she could—working in the cotton and soybean fields and waitressing. In 1971, she was considered one of the lucky blacks in our town when she landed a job as a shoe seamstress in nearby Charleston, Missouri, with the largest manufacturer in town, Brown Shoe Company—a company not known for its diversity at the time. The coveted and stable job with benefits meant her salary would increase to nearly $2 an hour. It was backbreaking, finger-numbing work that required bending over and pulling and stretching heavy fabrics, being careful not to pierce her finger with the

## Chapter 2: Uncover Your Why

giant needle—a repetitive motion that caused excruciating arthritis in her hands and back. Many evenings she'd ask one of us to rub her feet down in alcohol if the Epsom-salts foot bath didn't do the trick. Some nights when she thought we were asleep, I'd hear her crying out to the Lord, asking for help.

Momma was the daughter of a farmer, and she inherited the value of hard work from him. He plowed and worked his forty acres himself—excruciating work—from sunup to sundown. She passed down that work ethic to her children and set the example herself.

Mom had side-hustles in the 1950s, 1960s, and 1970s, long before it became a hashtag. Born in 1934, she was creative in supplementing her income. Mom had a huge garden: a 20-by-40-foot empty space next to our home where she'd raise food for us to eat, to sell, and to donate, and she raised farm animals in the backyard—all of which helped to feed her family.

Plagued by mounting bills and hungry mouths to feed, Mom knew how to stretch a dollar. Her weekly trips to the grocery store were mainly for essentials—milk, bread, and butter. We lived on maybe a dollar a day, pretty good for a woman raising so many children.

Despite her lot in life, Mom led by example. She was a tough as nails–strong, no-nonsense woman who had a thirst for knowledge. She was always trying to learn new ways to earn more money to feed her children. If she couldn't afford to buy something, she found a way to make it—or some semblance of it. I recognized her stress-filled face as she struggled endlessly, picking up part-time work at times to provide for ten girls and one boy on her own. Her tall, attractive exterior did not reveal the pressure-cooker life on which she managed to keep a lid every day.

It was her strong will, bravery, and the choices she made that altered our circumstances, but more than that, she taught me what I needed to transform my life, to move beyond poverty in a small town. She never let the fear of failure prevent her from moving forward. She held steadfastly to God's promises.

> *"For I know the plans I have for you," declares the* L<small>ORD</small>, *"plans to prosper you and not to harm you, plans to give you hope and a future."*
>
> **—Jeremiah 29:11** N<small>IV</small>

I was surrounded by poverty, but because of Mom's biblical teaching, I had the audacity to believe God's words in Jeremiah and pursue prosperity. At six years old, I wasn't sure how I would get there, but I would share with Momma my dreams of becoming an anchor—like my idol, CBS News legend Walter Cronkite. And someday I hoped to sit in the White House and interview the president of the United States.

When I look at my life today, after having fulfilled that dream, the hard work, the challenges and choices I have

*Chapter 2: Uncover Your Why*

made in my career, my relationship with how I spend, save, and use my money—so much of it is tied to my childhood experiences—the good and bad. And I bet the same is true of you.

## Hidden Trauma

While the financial circumstances you were born into might look somewhat different than mine, my guess is that those circumstances shaped your relationship with money. For those of us who find ourselves making poor choices around saving, spending, and earning money, the first step toward financial freedom is figuring out why we handle money as we do. It starts with looking at the past—and specifically, considering how money trauma rooted in childhood experiences might subconsciously affect the way we approach money today.

One of my biggest emotional traumas surrounding money happened when I was ten years old. I vividly recall the night I crept down the long, dark hallway of my childhood home. Headed to the bathroom, I could hear my mom having a late-night argument on the phone with someone. As I continued to tiptoe to the bathroom, she raised her voice angrily into the receiver: "So if I don't take you back, Romona doesn't get shoes?" Stunned, I stopped in my tracks and the floorboard creaked beneath my bare feet. Mom yelled out, "Who's there?" My heart racing, I did a light moonwalk in reverse back to my bed as quickly as I could.

Though I couldn't hear the other end of the conversation, I vowed that night I would never be reliant on anyone to buy me anything. I never spoke to Mom about what I overheard, fearing I'd get in trouble or blamed for eavesdropping. I buried the memory, unaware of its detrimental impact on my personal life, or the fact that I would carry that internal baggage within me for years.

At the time I wore shoes with three holes in them. During the winter, the snow and ice seeped through my shoes' soles—my feet becoming so painfully cold I surely thought I'd get frostbite. Mom had been promising me new shoes as soon as she got paid, but with every paycheck came another household emergency. Overhearing her conversation with the one whom I believed to be my father that night spawned deep resentment and anger—pain that would fuel my desire to work hard to lift myself out of poverty, and never be obligated to anyone.

What I didn't know was how that anger would manifest later in my life. When I started dating, when men would give me gifts, I would instinctively snap, "Why are you being so nice? What is this present for? What do you want?" I remember one guy saying, "Whoa, what did I do wrong? What's got you so uptight?" Of course, I didn't know that painful and demeaning moment of overhearing Mom's conversation was embedded deep within my soul. Because of it, I grew into an extremely independent woman. *It was my why*. It was a learned behavior, a coping mechanism I used not to feel beholden to anyone—and to ward off deep feelings of scarcity and insecurity.

*Chapter 2: Uncover Your Why*

> **REFLECTION POINT**
>
> Have you ever considered the concept of financial trauma before? Are there early experiences around money that you buried and moved on, telling yourself to be strong and not let it affect you?
>
> Research shows that these experiences do affect us subconsciously, but we may not realize it until something sparks those painful memories. And even then, we might not connect it to childhood trauma.
>
> Are there traumas in your past onto which you've been holding that have crippled how you value people, material things, or yourself? Feel free to jot them down.
>
> Can you pinpoint one or two "money traumas" that have hindered you from transforming your financial life?
>
> Are those experiences still a factor in how you show up in the world?

## Uncovering Old Lies

Until I started to write and pour over research for this book, I didn't even know there was a connection between childhood trauma and money. But it's been studied and documented; in fact, today there are even financial therapists available to help you heal from it.

Ed Coambs, a Charlotte-based marriage and family therapist, says financial therapy can help people recognize that experiences they had growing up, even experiences that may seem unrelated to money—such as their parents' divorce, an addiction, or some sort of assault or other trauma—might actually inform their financial habits on an subconscious level. Such adverse developmental experiences, he says, have a "profound impact on people," oftentimes for life. He notes that, "If you recognize that you have problematic financial behaviors and you've tried on your own to get them right and you haven't, a therapist can help you."[1]

Financial trauma can take many different shapes; often it is painful to unearth. Patricia, one of the women I interviewed, is a forty-two-year-old divorced mother of two. She shared with me that privately she calls herself things she would never allow anyone to say to her face. Horrible thoughts like, *You're fat; that's why your husband left you*, and *No one wants to love you*.

She also confided she has major debt, only saying it is mid-five figures. She admits she carries around a social inferiority complex. She tells a story of never feeling attractive, always battling weight loss, and craving acceptance, so she overcompensates with retail therapy. The compliments and admiration she gets from other women when wearing expensive clothes, especially shoes, make her feel special.

I asked her to think back to where those thoughts of needing acceptance might have originated. She hesitated,

---

[1] There's even an organization that can help you deal with financial trauma, The Financial Therapy Association: https://financialtherapyassociation.org/.

## Chapter 2: Uncover Your Why

then became cagey, only saying she knows exactly why but did not want to share. I could sense the emotion in her voice. I asked if she could share more, but she would only divulge that it was painful, and she'd prefer to keep it in the past. This is a common sentiment. Sadly, I don't think we can fully be whole and heal until we deal with the trauma and statements we believe about ourselves—things like, *You're not worthy; you'll never have enough; you can't let others help you;* or *you can't show weakness.* I believe those negative thoughts block God's plan to give you hope and a blessed future. For Patricia, these lies remain dormant until she's ready to spend money. Then they feed on her wallet, using those purchases to make her feel good about herself.

What you think of yourself is crucial to changing your money habits. It begins with being willing to ask yourself some tough questions about yourself.

National bestselling author and financial expert Rachel Cruz says, "When you take a closer look at your behavior and beliefs, money problems are usually just a symptom of a larger problem in your life."

> **REFLECTION POINT**
>
> Can you look below the surface and pinpoint money pains that still trigger you today?
>
> What would your finances look like if you started to heal from your money dysfunction?
>
> Are you willing to make a pledge right now to cultivate a healthier approach to handling your money?

## Changing the Narrative

It's safe to say my mom was probably not aware of the connection between childhood trauma and her tough-as-nails approach to raising her kids. She was a strict disciplinarian who insisted on knowing where her children were at all times. She was also as meticulous when it came to saving her money. Like many of you who are living paycheck to paycheck, working hard, and trying to make ends meet—you've probably not even thought about the role your younger years played in the money decisions you make today. You just do what you know needs to be done to get by.

Mom often talked about her childhood. The trauma of losing her beloved father at the age of twelve dramatically changed the course of her young life. Her relationship with her mother was strained, so she searched for the love she felt was missing in her life, but that search brought

## Chapter 2: Uncover Your Why

her heartache and pain. Men often made promises, but they walked in and out of her life as she struggled to raise her eleven children.

When you live in poverty, it can grab hold of you, constraining your options, until it's got you completely in its power. It will drown your thoughts of ever achieving upward mobility—slowly chipping away at an untested mindset, dashing dreams, even pushing you to the point of giving up. But Mom never gave up.

Blessed with godly wisdom and discernment, she led by example. She always shared the Scriptures with us. Mom raised me to believe that God can improve your situation if you believe in Him and give Him the glory. She mentally prepared her children to block out negative thoughts of *I can't* or *I never will*, because *God can*. It was engrained in us that we should be strong and courageous and never let anyone take advantage of us. Mom encouraged us to speak up for ourselves, especially when we were treated unfairly.

Although my mother had suffered her own money trauma, and even though she lived in poverty, she began to change the narrative in her own life and in the lives of her children. When she wasn't working, she stayed home with her kids. There was no clubbing; in fact, there was very little socializing. She would just watch the news and read her Bible. Clutching the big burgundy, worn-looking Book, her face would light up as she became engrossed in God's words. She had scrawled so many notes in her

Bible and underlined countless Scriptures that she needed duct tape to hold it together.

In its pages, she escaped the financial chokehold that restrains many of us. Her faith in God brought comfort in her everyday struggles and fear. Lessons on prosperity and purpose helped her to push forward and believe that better days were ahead. She never waited for the government to rescue her. She saved what little she could scrape together, and she refused to live off welfare even when those around her said she should. Mom felt she had birthed us into the world, and it was her job to care for us. The small amount of food aid she accepted from the government helped us get by, but her tireless work is what sustained us. Mom armed herself with wisdom—the kind that is God-fed, full of faith and fight, and brings blessings along the way.

At the heart of our faith-filled life was our church attendance. Mom would sashay down the aisle to the collection plate every Sunday—giving her monetary blessing to the church. "Momma, you sure was twisting in church today," we'd say, giggling. She'd swear it was her natural walk, that her hips and legs just had a mind of their own.

Armed with our pennies, all seven of us at the time eagerly awaited our turn to put our own money in the collection plate so we could give back to God. Those were my first lessons of always giving back a portion of what you earned. Mom didn't ever skip a Sunday of giving. At times, I'd hear her complain there just wasn't enough

## Chapter 2: Uncover Your Why

to put anything in the offering plate, but somehow she'd always scrounge up something. Despite her situation, she was a faithful giver, believing she would reap great rewards from God.

There was a lot of joy to be found in our tiny church in Wyatt, Missouri, right across Highway 57 and about two miles down the road from our house. Holy Grove Baptist Church is where I learned to love the Lord. Mom made sure we were drenched in the Word of Jesus. We were required to attend church quite frequently—Sunday school, Sunday services, Bible studies, revivals. It was our second home. The Word of God was engrained in me.

I should be ashamed to admit that my favorite times were after the services, because hunger can cloud your judgment even when you're praising God. After church, we'd all gather in the church basement, where the small kitchen was crammed with three small tables. That is where the mothers of the church would prepare meals for the sick and shut-ins—along with enough to feed the entire congregation. Miss Elsie's homemade apple pie was always served fresh out of the oven, with its aroma oozing into the air—tart, fresh apples, cinnamon, and buttery, golden, flaky crust crimped around the edges. When your nose got a whiff of the fried chicken and barbecued ribs, you began to walk like a zombie, slowly and blindly being led toward the overpowering smell. Mashed potatoes were piled high, with a stick of butter on top slowly melting into the piping-hot, fluffy white delight. I can still see all the open containers of mismatched bowls and cleaned-out chitlins buckets filled with gallons of potato salad, collard and turnip greens, squash, and the best buttermilk corn bread you've ever tasted—made with potent spoiled milk. I always wanted the corner pieces with the buttery, crusty, crumbling edges!

The Sunday fixings were more than just great food. They were lessons from God's people that we share what we have. And those memories are a reminder to me that even out of difficult circumstances, God can bring forth wholeness, goodness, and the hope of better days. In that church, seeds were planted that would stay with me throughout my life, especially as I began to plow my own path to prosperity.

*Chapter 2: Uncover Your Why*

## REFLECTION POINT

If you're struggling right now with your finances, stop saying you'll never be free of your money issues. In your head, your fear of never getting ahead, of never paying off the student loan or credit card debt, might be warring with your faith. Mental anguish and suffering are not God's will for our lives. Our heavenly Father doesn't want us struggling, barely getting by, unable to support ourselves and our families. I discovered His plan to prosper me hinged greatly on my belief and trust in Him and His promises. Try changing the narrative and start believing you *can* dig yourself out. I believe that fear and trauma, some big and some small, can stunt your growth toward a life of financial independence.

No matter your financial situation, allow hard times to motivate you and learn how your burdens can grow bravery in you. The biggest naysayer is the one inside your own head. Block out the voice that says you will never be prosperous, the whispers that say you had money, but now, look at you—you're broke. When you focus on the life you don't have, that negative energy can make you bitter, and you will stop believing and dreaming about a better tomorrow.

*Jesus looked at them and said, "With man this is impossible, but with God all things are possible."*
—**Matthew 19:26** NIV

The world will make you believe your dreams of prosperity are impossible, because of your race, social status, or class—yet just as my mom gave my siblings and me permission to dream, you also have the same permission to dream. Nothing is impossible if we are willing to work for it, trust God, and learn.

CHAPTER 3

# YOU DON'T KNOW WHAT YOU DON'T KNOW

Even with Mom's teachings about what our lives could become, we were still children, somewhat influenced by our peers and especially what we saw on television. Because of what I watched on TV, I thought only white people could be rich. After all, they were the only people I saw on TV with lots of beautiful things. I loved singing along as the theme song came on to my favorite show: *Gilligan's Island*: "The millionaire and his wife, the movie star . . ." Ginger was always impeccably dressed, and the Howells were a hoot with their upper-crust manners.

So, I get it. When you don't have a lot, and someone tells you to just save and do the right thing with your money, financial freedom might seem unattainable. However, I know from experience, it's not how much you earn that brings you financial success. Trust me, if you start saving your money—whatever amount you can—one day that money will save you from whatever hardship you face.

My first memory of earning money harkens back to helping my grandma Viola straighten up her house. After I was done, she'd nudge me to run to the kitchen, look in the lower cupboard, and bring her the large Campbell's tomato soup can, to get the nickel or sometimes the dime that I'd earned. Breathless with excitement and powered by my pudgy little legs, I would make a beeline to the kitchen, knowing what was inside that jar. Only five years old, and still not in complete control of my body, I was meticulous, making sure the contents of the can didn't spill out all over the kitchen floor as it had a few times before.

Earning a dime at Grandma's house was a big payday for a child who only got a little more money years later when my siblings and I would go on money hunts—one of our favorite pastimes. You may have to be from the South to know what "money hunts" are. I'm told a group of bored, poverty-stricken boys in Alabama started the game.

Ideally, for the hunt we needed dry conditions, clear skies, and preferably a bright sun, hot against our faces and illuminating our path. The soil needed to be the right consistency, too—hardened enough to see cracks or divots in the ground, making it easier to spot the shiny jewels. It was a ritual every Saturday in the summer months. Like hawks hovering up above tracking their prey below, my

## Chapter 3: You Don't Know What You Don't Know

sister Evonne and I would walk down the dirt road with our eyeballs locked on the claylike soil, looking for lost change.

Of all my nine sisters, Evonne was my first-choice partner for the money hunts. She was a master at hitting the jackpot. At nine, she was a year older than me, and we made a great team. And she was not afraid of anything—not the stray animals nor the slithering snakes we might encounter along the road. Her job was also to scare the living daylights out of any kid who homed in on our territory. We couldn't let anyone know we were so poor we had to hunt for money.

I was just the opposite of Evonne—afraid of everything. I was the big, chubby girl, five-foot-five and toting just north of eighty pounds at eight years old. I was more interested in books and figuring out how to creatively make money to buy the candy we craved. Still, in the money games, my job was to scout the area where we were most likely to find the loot. Since most people walked on the right side of the road, that's where most of their money would fall.

First, we needed tools: sticks the length of a cane, but half the thickness; brown grocery bags; and our tennis shoes for the one-mile dirt road trek. Then we were ready. We scavenged down the dusty road, searching for the loose change that mostly old folks dropped while walking home. Those coins were like buried treasure, just waiting for someone to discover them. On a good day, we'd score a dollar. Not-so-good days netted maybe a quarter or so.

It was not difficult to spot the shiny, new coins. The sunlight usually danced off the copper or silver mints. Older ones were often embedded in the dried mud, barely peeking out from the earth. That's when we'd we'd use our cane-like stick and unearth them, using our fingernails to dig them out and then rub away all the dirt and grime stuck in its crevices. Sometimes we'd use a little spit and wipe them clean on our clothes—that made them as good as new.

Next, we'd turn our attention to the ditches, searching for our other pot of gold—pop bottles. There were no trash cans along the road, so people often discarded their soda bottles wherever they saw fit. We collected dirty, grimy, soil-stained bottles. The six-inch gems were usually buried underneath a mountain of debris in the ditches. Gnats and flies hovering over dumped banana and orange peels, along with snack wrappers, sticks, and dead leaves, often made the treasure hard to spot. Coca-Cola, Pepsi, Dr Pepper—they all spelled money. One bottle would fetch us two cents at the store. On a good day, we'd find about ten of the glass gems. They were only accepted clean, so at home we'd run hot water over them to dissolve the mud and crud. Later we would carefully place them in a grocery bag to trade and then evenly split the profits.

Our money hunts were a lot of work, but each week, they allowed us to afford the giant, pink, one-cent bubble gum, red-hot jawbreakers, and potato chips. If we were

## Chapter 3: You Don't Know What You Don't Know

really lucky, we could buy our favorite, more expensive treats: PayDay and Butterfinger candy bars.

I didn't realize it then, but I was learning valuable lessons about working to earn money and saving some for later.

When scarcity is all you've ever known, there is a lot you don't know—especially when it comes to money. As I think back on my childhood, I recognize the important lessons that were imparted to me by my grandmother. Her wisdom was limited by our circumstances, though, and there was still so much I would come to learn over time.

My grandmother shared cautionary tales about making sure my money was secure. Sometimes she instructed me to fetch her paper money. "Go back there in my bedroom, lift up my mattress, and brang me five dollahs."

Like many black people of her time, she watched her parents, who were born in the 1870s, keep their savings safe—in their homes. She, too, would keep her money tucked under her mattress—and she had good reason, one of the biggest being a lack of trust.

In 1865, President Abraham Lincoln signed the Freedman's Bank Act, authorizing the opening of a bank for recently emancipated slaves. Within almost a decade, the Freedman's bank deposits at its thirty-four U.S. branches totaled more than $3 million (about $65 million in today's dollars).

In 1874, under a shroud of rumors and corruption

within the bank's all-white management, the bank closed. Most depositors lost their savings, receiving little to no money back from the bank or the federal government.

The purpose of the bank was to help newly freed African Americans become more financially stable and expand their access to capital—in turn improving the financial security of those least fortunate. Instead, their life savings were either stolen or grossly mismanaged.

"When they found out that they had lost, or been swindled out of all their savings," said Booker T. Washington, "they lost faith in savings banks, and it was a long time after this before it was possible to mention a savings bank for Negroes without some reference being made to the disaster of [the Freedmen's Bank]."

So, most black Americans like my grandma, who had been traumatized by the ordeal, felt their money was safer hidden in their homes than leaving it with a stranger for safekeeping. She didn't trust the banks, and I don't know if she ever overcame that mistrust in financial institutions.

As a result, my grandmother taught me how to hide and safekeep my money. But there were things she could not teach me when it came to financial literacy, and it would take me a long time to learn what I didn't know.[2]

---

[2] This is such an incredible story that can't be told in a few paragraphs. I encourage you to read more about the history of the Freedman's Bank. Start here: https://www.treasury.gov/connect/blog/Pages/Freedmans-Savings-Bank.aspx.

*Chapter 3: You Don't Know What You Don't Know*

## Learn What You Don't Know

Mom was different. Although her own mother didn't trust banks, Mom was a disciplined saver and she deposited her money in the bank. When I was seven years old, I was pretty good in math and excellent at reading. Sometimes, when Mom was exhausted, she would call on me to fill out her yellow bank deposit slip for five bucks—if she was lucky, sometimes a few dollars more—for her savings account each month. I would eagerly write out the bank ledger deposit. There were months when she moaned at having so little saved; other times, she thanked God for an extra two or three dollars she could sock away. She called it her "money for hard times," and she encouraged me to always put money back for troubled times.

Even when I was in second grade, Mom wanted me to understand how unexpected tough times can fall on you, times when you'd need extra help to make it through. I can still see her eyebrows raised and hear her stern voice, explaining how even a little savings would grow into a lot more if it was left in the bank untouched.

I didn't quite understand all the financial terms, but I got the gist of it. I watched her leave to make the six-mile trip to town on the first of each month to run errands and deposit her savings. If I was lucky, I got to accompany her. I marveled at the rapport she had with the all-white bankers. There was an air of respectability in their exchanges. The bank manager would shake her hand, and all the tellers knew her by name. Mom had a gift, a sweet way of winning over folks who might otherwise have shunned blacks back then. It was my first introduction to one of the rare places that seemed to make Mom the happiest. A smile would cross her face when she walked into the building, and she carried a sense of pride as she explained to me, "This is the place where I deposit my money, where it will grow."

Many months, money was so tight, but she always managed to eke out something to save. Looking back, I am amazed that my mother could save and even prosper on a $2-an-hour wage. I can't recall how much she had put away when I left home for college, but I never remember her missing a monthly deposit.

Mom was determined to raise her children on her own after my dad and stepdad walked in and then out of her life. A God-fearing woman, she always stressed that it wasn't a good look for a grown person to always beg and borrow from other people for money: "The wicked borrows but does not pay back, but the righteous is generous and gives" (Psalm 37:21 ESV). If she borrowed, she paid back her debts. She implored us never to ask anyone for anything we could earn ourselves.

Mom pushed us to believe the cycle of poverty that plagued generations of our family could be broken. It was a mammoth goal, but she was a woman of tremendous faith. She did have a support system to help make ends meet—her children. We helped around the house and

## Chapter 3: You Don't Know What You Don't Know

worked every summer to make extra money.

Most of Mom's adult work life consisted of struggling on a low-wage salary. Before she was hired at the factory, she spent a short time at a nursing home, and she also cleaned houses. Our tiny home was filled with difficult days and prayer-filled nights. I don't remember how many times we warmed our bodies over the electric stove because there was no heat, and I remember sleepless nights as I listened to Mom crying out to God, begging Him to provide a financial increase for our family.

Through it all, though, she believed—and lived out—the wisdom in the Bible that says, "Lazy men are soon poor; hard workers get rich" (Proverbs 10:4 TLB).

No one could ever have described Mom as lazy. She worked hard for every dollar she got, and then she worked hard again to stretch those dollars to cover our needs. Even though she lived paycheck to paycheck, she never let poverty define her. She refused to accept that living poor was all there was for her life. Her faith taught her that if she was wise and saved some money, she could build a better life for her and her kids.

To this day, her work ethic has rivaled that of anyone I've ever met. How she worked every day, cared for her children, tended to her garden, and ran a small animal farm in our backyard was incredible to witness—and it was an essential model for me as I began to pursue my own path to prosperity and true wealth.

## Mom's Money Lessons

In 2016, I interviewed Mom about her life for my memoir, *A Dirt Road to Somewhere*. I asked her why she pushed her kids to pursue higher education and plow our own path to a more prosperous life since she had only gotten through ninth grade at that time. (Later, in 2002, at the age of sixty-eight, she earned her GED–and at seventy, she entered college, majoring in computer science! Unfortunately, she was sidelined by a hip injury in her sophomore year.)

Mom said she initially got the idea from one of her toughest jobs: working for Mr. McKay, a wealthy widower with three adolescent sons. She was their housecleaner and caregiver. It was a tough job, made tougher because the boys' rooms were always a cluttered, grimy mess. Their mother had died of cancer at forty-two years of age, and their father worked ten-hour days. He mostly barked orders at his sons from downstairs for not picking up after themselves. Mom ended up quitting that job after a year because the minimal amount of pay didn't make up for the heavy workload. However, while there, she gained some valuable lessons about the correlation between a higher education and prosperity, and she wisely adopted Mr. McKay's money principles and passed them on to her kids.

Her never-give-up attitude was adopted from her father, but the rich man's conversations with his sons intrigued

## Chapter 3: You Don't Know What You Don't Know

her. As the boys gathered for breakfast each morning, Mr. McKay would ask if they had done their homework, and he disciplined them sternly if any of them were not achieving their potential.

"Do you think that because we are well off, you can slack off at school?" He'd frown across the table. "Don't think you're going to live off my money forever! You're expected to go to school, go to college, and then take over this business. You will make something of yourselves and earn your own money. Do you hear me, sons?" he'd bark.

Each day Mom listened as Mr. McKay taught his sons about money and success. She absorbed these financial and educational lessons and mixed them with her own verbiage. She closely watched a successful person, adopted his wisdom, brought it back to her nest, and mentally nourished her babies with it. Her translation was a little more colorful than his, but the same principles applied.

## Rich Man's Lessons

*Rich Man:* You will not be failures.

*Mom*: I ain't raisin' no dummies.

*Rich Man:* Sons, I want you to learn the value of a dollar and what it takes to run this household.

*Mom:* It takes a lot of money to take care of y'all, so learn somethin' at that school.

*Rich Man:* We have to be prudent in our spending to afford your college costs.

*Mom:* You gotta work summer jobs and help save for your college education.

*Rich Man:* Hang with kids who are going somewhere, who are from good families.

*Mom:* Stay away from those bad a%$$ kids who ain't goin' nowhere.

*Rich Man:* Education is a must if you're going to run our family business someday.

*Mom:* You can make somethin' of yourself if you go to college.

*Rich Man:* Your mom and I have an inheritance saved for each of you.

*Mom:* I got nothin' saved up for y'all yet, but I'm tryin'.

*Rich Man:* You are never too young to start planning for your future.

*Mom:* You want somethin' different out of life, you gotta think on it now.

In addition to Mr. McKay's lessons, most of Mom's lessons were built on the bedrock of her own wisdom and discernment, rooted in Scripture: "Wisdom is a shelter as money is a shelter, but the advantage of knowledge is this: Wisdom preserves those who have it" (Eccl. 7:12 NIV). Some of these lessons included:

- Always put God first and "do thangs His way."

## Chapter 3: You Don't Know What You Don't Know

Trust Him to fight your battles.

- Don't let nobody tell you what you can't do because of where you come from. We're all the same in God's eyes.
- Don't spend all your money on junk food and them cassettes and CDs; put some o' that money in the bank. (This was her favorite.)

Mom didn't use the most eloquent words, but they were hers, and the message was delivered and retained.

Also, Mom never succumbed to a woe-is-me mentality. She lived in scarcity, yet she always trusted she could accumulate more. What she didn't know, she learned. She loved striking up conversations with the people she did business with, learning and soaking up their knowledge on how she could get ahead.

She lived out Maya Angelou's words: "Do the best you can until you know better. Then when you know better, do better."

I was raised to do better, to think of a life beyond our circumstances.

If you are struggling to figure out the next steps in your finances, I hope this chapter encourages and inspires you. Don't convince yourself you should be content with your circumstances and settle because of what you don't know. Maybe you feel intimidated by learning about investing or paying off debt, but you can't start to heal from that fear if you're not willing to do the work. Saying "I don't know how" is not an excuse. With the internet, we have a wealth of information at our fingertips.

No matter the amount of your take-home pay, start learning about saving, investing, and financial independence. If you have children, start talking about money with your kids. Those conversations can change their lives. Mom never tried to camouflage our lack of money. She taught us with both her words and her actions how to live within our means, as well as to save, plan, and have a vision for the future.

As I grew older, my dreams of a better life grew, as well. Even if I didn't make it from poverty to prosperity, I was raised with the mindset that everything I needed to prosper was within me with the help of Christ.

## Chapter 3: You Don't Know What You Don't Know

### REFLECTION POINT

Learning what you don't know is one of the keys to healing from financial trauma. Part of that means seeking help when you need it—whether from a financial therapist, a trusted mentor, or financial advisors who can guide you on how to manage your money. But there are also some mindset adjustments you can begin to make right now. I've made these over the course of my own journey, and I encourage you to apply them to your own situation.

- First, be aware that you have a problem with money.

- Admit that the way you've always handled your finances is not working and be willing to adopt new money habits.

- Begin to identify any lies you might be telling yourself about your money, your value, and your future.

- Refuse to let old narratives or other people tell your mind who you are. Just because the world viewed me as a poverty-stricken statistic, I didn't have to wear that label.

- If you're living in the pain of never getting ahead, do not ignore the hurt. Instead, embrace it, use it, and learn from it.

- Practice gratitude, no matter your financial mistakes.

CHAPTER 4

# THE GIFT THAT KEEPS ON GIVING

Not all my money lessons were based on hardships. Even today, the positive lessons I learned still play a significant role in my life. The way I see people, how I share my personal stories, how I move about this nation, my willingness to help others—all of it stems from the gifts I received from others as a child. I'm not referring to monetary gifts, but to the intangible ones that shape your beliefs. The ones that build character in you. The spiritual teachings that produce faith and your view of the world. How kindness begets kindness. How being surrounded by hardship and hard work births perseverance.

If you take a moment right now to think back, can you remember someone who had a major impact on your own life: mentally, educationally, or even monetarily?

For me, two special ladies come to mind.

I can hear Mom's elderly friends sitting on their front

porch practicing songs from their hymnals, preparing to sing in the church choir on Sunday. Mom would send me to make a delivery of fresh eggs from our hens to our friends Misses Gloria and Elsie. In our community, the barter system helped to make ends meet, especially when jobs were scarce. Just about everybody shared something they had. I learned at a young age to help my senior neighbors and not to expect to be paid for my efforts. What I earned for free from the two of them was a world of opportunity through books. Before I was old enough to make Mom's food deliveries, I would scavenge my neighbor's trash for any old, damaged books she would throw away. Some were pasted with food, or they had grease stains or missing pages, but that was fine with me. I'd also find some gems that looked fairly new. I loved reading like I loved breathing. I could get lost in a story and become whoever I wanted to be. The nearest library was six miles away in the next town. It was too far to walk, and with Mom always at work, we never got to visit.

Miss Elsie was a former elementary teacher's aide, and she had dozens of worn and torn discarded books from the school. I had no books at home because we weren't allowed to take any out of the school. In my then-all-black school, there was a book shortage, and we had to share any books we had with other students. But Miss Elsie owned a pile of childhood classics, including *Little Red Riding Hood*, *The Three Little Pigs*, and *Jack and the Beanstalk*.

## Chapter 4: The Gift That Keeps on Giving

Elsie and Gloria were deeply religious women. They were in their seventies but still spry in body and mind. They loved to rock back and forth in their rockers, usually on the porch, with the Holy Spirit coursing through their bodies like a swift wind before an impending storm. Sometimes I would walk up to the porch during a prayer, and Miss Gloria sounded like she was from our native homeland speaking in tongues, a language regarded as one of the gifts of the Holy Spirit. It used to scare me. She almost looked like a witch, possessed. Her head twisted sideways; her cloudy, aging gray eyes cocked; her hands were lifted in the air, and she'd start speaking so fast in words I couldn't understand.

Gloria was a tough old woman—no-nonsense, skinny, with long, *long* gray hair that graced her backside. She was partially crippled, with shoulders that curved forward and a permanent hump in her back. She was aided by a cane to get around. She would speak to you from the side, as she was unable to lift her head or neck very high. There were various rumors about the cause of her physical features, all of which were a little frightening.

She might have been a bit scary, but she was my hero. Once she beat a boy across his back with her cane after he violently shoved me in a ditch in front of her house. I had refused to give up the candy I had worked so hard for, and Jimmy was determined to take it. "Run on home to yo momma, gal!" she yelled at me as she continued clubbing Jimmy. His hands were in the air as he tried to defend himself from the blows of that cane. Gloria also once witnessed a stray dog that had given chase, nipping at my heels as I walked home, and she yelled for me to take shelter in her house.

Elsie was the white-haired, outspoken one, with an eye and ear for what she called "devilment"—or a person who was up to no good. A large woman with a big bosom, she'd hug you so tight you'd face-plant in the middle of her colorful, floral dresses, smothered by a strong whiff of her sweet-fragranced perfume. She forbade us kids from walking behind her because she didn't like how her backside wobbled when she walked.

"Chil', don't you ever get fat! These hips and behind won't ever stop followin' you."

I especially loved making Mom's deliveries to these ladies because in addition to the loose change and the books I'd receive, they'd always ask if I was hungry and wanted something to eat. Mom forbade us from asking or begging anyone for food, but if it was offered, I would gladly take it.

"I know yo momma havin' it hard, feedin' all y'all. Run in der and get yo'self a few cookies I baked and some milk—and grab a book, too," said a smiling Elsie.

Next to her kitchen table was an unstable wooden shelf with a mishmash overflow of books. She kept them for whenever her grandkids visited, but she always offered me a few to keep because she loved watching my hunger

## Chapter 4: The Gift That Keeps on Giving

for knowledge, along with the curiosity I had for literary adventures. I feared Mom would not take kindly to me taking a gift, so the books were reserved for my bimonthly food deliveries.

Mom had shared with Elsie my dream of becoming a journalist—like my idol, Walter Cronkite—a dream I'd had since I was six years old. Elise also understood that as a middle child with ten siblings, I didn't get much attention. Because I was a good kid who did what she was told and got good grades, Mom's attention was rarely on me; it was always focused on the children who were getting in trouble at school. But Elsie filled in that motherly gap by providing doses of inspiration and introducing me to a world of possibilities through books.

I especially remember being engrossed in the book *The Giving Tree*. The story reminded me of the generous people who surrounded me—as well as the kind of person I never wanted to grow up to be. It's the tale of an apple tree that loves a boy. The tree sacrifices everything for his friend, but when the boy becomes a man, his wants and needs increase. He pursues the trappings of money and possessions and becomes very selfish. At first, I thought, *What a mean and ungrateful person*, but the story also taught me a lot about unconditional love and helping others.

Miss Elsie loved to give to others. Each bite of her sugar cookies was a taste of kindness, from a woman who had nothing to gain from her generosity. That was a lesson

I would take with me on my journey to a better life. At Miss Elsie's house, I learned that kindness is when you do something for someone who doesn't have the ability to do anything for you in return.

Back outside on the porch, Elsie and Gloria would talk mostly about God and gratitude. They never missed an opportunity to deliver words of wisdom that would later serve me well. Gloria was my protector; Elsie, my motivator.

"How you fairin' up dere at that school?" Elsie said, lowering her head and peering up from her glasses. "Yo momma say you smart. You keep doin' good, you hear? We ain't never had nothing, we never finished school, but you stay in dem books and stay away from dem mannish boys, and you showly will make somethin' of yo'self. The world is different now, you got some opportunities. You worth somethin', gal. Don't you forget it."

Back then, the jumbled sentences and broken words didn't mean much, but as I grew older, I recognized them as the tremendous gifts they were. I could easily translate: Always study hard, pursue my education, and I would have great value in the world. I also realize they were a part of God's blessing to give me hope and a future.

In this chapter, I invite you to think back on your own life. Were you taught that you have value in this world? That no matter your background, whether it was one of means or scarcity, financial success was possible for you?

*Chapter 4: The Gift That Keeps on Giving*

*Prosperity* was never a word I heard uttered in my community, but poverty was a great teacher. It taught me to value the little things, to make the best of what I have and to never stop fighting hard for more. My childhood was filled with economic insecurity and emotional despair, but my neighbors cared whether I made it or not, and loving God was a huge part of that.

My little enclave didn't have a mall, a movie theater, or even fast-food restaurants, but what we did have was a community of caring people who would give you the shirt off their back if you were in need.

Today children are carpooled to different activities at a hectic pace and bombarded with social media. I now know there were great benefits growing up in rural middle America. The slow, quiet pace I thought was boring gave me a sense of passion, love, and respect for people, animals, and the environment. In that struggling community, the blessings of my faith, character, and strong work ethic were built.

That community is also where God offered me help through the generosity of others.

I did not know it then but emerging from tremendous scarcity would serve me well throughout my life.

## The Final Gift

Ten years later, my visit home to Wilson City after graduating from college would be the last time I'd see

Miss Elsie. Miss Gloria had died a few years prior.

"Come on in here, gal! Let me take a look at you." She stood in her doorway, holding the screen open for me to enter her home.

When I approached, I gave her a warm but gentle embrace.

She was now in her mid-eighties, and the years had not been kind. She wore a worn and weary exterior—a fatigued look that told the tale of a life lived harder than it should have been. Her smile still stretched across much of her now-wrinkled face, each line telling a story of hardship, joy, and gratitude for just livin'.

"Yo momma said you just graduated. That's real good. I knowed you could do it. Let's sit in the house a bit." I walked past the rocking chairs where she and Miss Gloria had once been fixtures, canvassing the road and singing to God. The chairs were now gray, dry-rotted wood, filled with splinters.

Elsie walked predictably slow for someone in failing health, like her brain was struggling to tell each foot how to take a step.

"Come on now, what I tell ya 'bout walkin' behind me," she barked. I smiled, but I realized she was all skin and bones now, with no sign of the big hips and behind she used to tote around.

She was a ghost of a woman, so frail it looked like it hurt her just to walk. Sickness had visibly ravaged her

## Chapter 4: The Gift That Keeps on Giving

body. It hadn't affected her mind, though; she was as feisty as ever.

My eyes settled on the interior of her home. Not much had changed since I was a kid, except everything was now much older and worse for wear. The same lace dinette tablecloth, the familiar faux fur thrown over her sofa, a four-by-four piece of plywood covering the caved-in area in front of the fridge.

"Evonne, is that you?" she asked, now relaxing in her sunken-in living room chair. She had covered the seat with a bed pillow. I guess the springs had given way.

"No, Miss Elsie, it's me, Romona," I smiled. "You still confuse me with my sister."

"I know my eyesight ain't the best no mo. Yo voice is different, that's how I knowed it's you. I went to the stoh yesterday. Y'all gals look alike."

Her words and thoughts kept running together and changing in midsentence as she struggled to stay on message.

"I got somethin' fo ya. I put some thangs aside 'cause I knowed you was comin' home. Reach under that cushion of my couch where you sittin'. Pull that green pouch out from the corna of that couch. Dig yo hand deep down in there."

Forcing my hand between the couch cushions and moving it back and forth, I felt a ropelike string, and I grabbed it and gave it a good yank.

"What is it?" I curiously asked, holding what felt like paper and coins inside a felt pouch.

"Henrutta said you don't have a job yet and you scraping to get by. Look in dere and get yo'self somethin'."

"Oh no, I couldn't, Miss Elsie. You need your money," I insisted as I looked around at the same furniture I'd see in her house since grade school.

There was probably eight dollars and some change in the pouch. I smiled, thinking, *Some of my people are still hiding their money in crevices and under couch cushions.*

"Take two or three dollas of that, hun."

"Oh no, I can't," I graciously responded. It was true that I was struggling without a job and living with my sister, but I was a young, able-bodied adult, and no way was I taking an old woman's last dime.

Elsie slowly rose from her chair as I rushed to help her stand. She went into her bedroom and then emerged with a set of what looked like used sheets and mismatched pillowcases. She put these on her coffee table, next to a pile of what I could see was silver shine peeking out from a dry dishrag in which they were wrapped. It was a few assorted utensils—dinner spoons, forks, and butter knives. They were worn, some slightly bent, a sign they had more than served their purpose.

"One mo thang. The ladies at the church, we all made this fo you," she said as her eyes focused on a large black garbage bag on the floor next to her coffee table.

## Chapter 4: The Gift That Keeps on Giving

The top of it was tied in a knot. "Go on, open it," she instructed. Anticipation filled my heart as I tried to guess what the church women had done for me. Inside was a hand-stitched patchwork quilt. It had ten-by-ten pieces of different fabric stitched together into a queen-sized bedcover. "We all found as many scraps of material as we could and sewed you this. It will keep you warm. We ain't got much, but I wanted to make sho you got somethin' fo graduatin'. I wish I had mo to give."

The quilt had been lovingly stitched in a rainbow of colors. Each square pattern, print, and hue had been hand-sewn together, perfectly providing cozy memories of my people and their passions. It was a gift that would remind me of the selfless charity of the poor. I would take with me the warmth of these women to shield my body from the winter's cold, and it did just that in my first apartment through my first home.

Tears escaped my eyes as I thought about their labor of love. People with so little had wanted desperately to help another.

The book of Proverbs spells it out. These women had wisdom, and they knew the Word of God, which says, "He who is generous will be blessed, for he gives some of his food to the poor" (Prov. 22:9 NASB).

That was my community. Many knew they might never achieve financial security in their lives, but they were determined to support the children of the community who had a shot at a more prosperous life. It's the way the Bible teaches us to live.

Memories of Elsie conjure up so many beautiful thoughts in my mind as I write this book. The pages and pages of books she allowed me to read sparked my curiosity and ignited my imagination about a world of opportunity outside my town. I wish she and her friend Gloria had lived to see the gift of their seeds planted in my memory and in my heart. It truly has been a gift that keeps on giving.

# PART 2
# RESET YOUR MONEY MINDSET

CHAPTER 5

# THE POOR, THE RICH, AND WHAT'S POSSIBLE

By now, you should understand "why and what" motivates you to spend. You are connecting the dots and starting to identify specific areas in which you can improve. For me, I had to stop the idea that I needed to spend money to maintain my public image. It was just a charade. My mom used to always say that if you want to know what you look like, you should just look in the mirror; you don't have to rely on other people's opinions. So, when I truly started to look in the mirror, I realized I could look just as good in a $100 dress on sale as I could in a dress for which I had paid $700 full price. I won't lie—sometimes on rare occasions, that $700 dress was worth it, but I only paid that much for a dress when I could afford it.

The truth is, even before I left home for college, my financial mindset was beginning to take shape. My mom had been drilling in my head that our dire surroundings shouldn't diminish my dreams of prosperity. However, growing up in poverty was like wearing an overly weighted backpack—you felt the heaviness of it every day because of the opportunities and access you didn't have. But I was determined that the extra load would not hold me back. I ached for a more prosperous life, and I dreamed of how I would get there. But those dreams only came true because I refused to accept the limitations others tried to place on me.

In late May 1977, I took a summer job at Brown Shoe Company, where my mom worked. I wanted to earn some money before I headed off to college in the fall.

The shoe factory was the largest employer in Charleston, Missouri—a nearby town of six thousand people. The company was the maker of the well-known Buster Brown line of shoes for children and later for women.

To picture Charleston, think of Mayberry in the 1960s sitcom *The Andy Griffith Show*—quaint, quiet, with a main street flanked by about two dozen mom-and-pop stores. In front of Waggener's Sinclair gas station was the "Liar's Bench," where fisherman and hunters were said to gather to tell tales of their unbelievable catches of the day. It was also where people confessed their deepest, darkest sins, never to be shared again.

Inside the Brown Shoe Company, a dozen sights and sounds of grinding, bobbing, thumping, and clicking rang out—even in my memory today. The first time I walked

## Chapter 5: The Poor, the Rich, and What's Possible

into the brown-reddish one-story brick building was intimidating.

The massive interior space was alive with the voices of 150 workers. Slightly warped, creaky wood floors announced the comings and goings with soft clicks and thumps of footsteps moving about.

The *chuka, chuka, chuka* of noisy sewing machines roared through the plant as large industrial needles punched through heavy-duty fabrics. The air was filled with the smell of textiles, leather, rubber, oil, and glue; combined, a musty odor filled my nostrils. Giant ceiling spotlights along the assembly lines beamed down, lighting up the equipment and ensuring accuracy in making the perfect shoe.

One of the most skilled, top stitcher's mother sat a few rows from me—sewing the soles on the shoes. The backbreaking, finger-numbing work would leave her hands in excruciating pain by quitting time. They put me in the finishing section of the plant—in packaging. My job was to check the quality of the shoes as they came down the conveyor belt, a simple job that eliminated any chance I'd lose a finger on the sewing machines.

Working in that factory was one of the last times I was fully immersed in the poverty-stricken town where I grew up, and it was one of the first times I began to see it with adult eyes—eyes that were already seeing a future take place beyond this town.

## Poor Girl, Rich Life

As I think about the people I worked with there, the country twang of the rural poor still lingers in my ear. People who said "hun" instead of "honey." "Yes'm," not "yes, ma'am," or "sir." Words and phrases like "y'all," and "I ain't got," and "I'm finna do somethin'," echoed throughout the plant daily.

There were eight adults on my line, all with quirky and strong personalities, each with gut-busting and dire stories to tell. Some names and faces I can hardly recall, but Ethel June and Bobby Jo's stories are embedded in my brain. I talked to these two coworkers daily for five months. Most days the area was thick with tension over their financial plight—other times, laughter rang out harmoniously. The two had been positioned a few feet away, assigned to teach me the inspection process.

They were a chatty duo. Ethel June was a colorful character—a short, freckled-face, stout woman with blue eyes and powder-blue eyeshadow. Her long, black, spiderlike eyelashes indicated her love of mascara. She drew on thick, black eyeliner to a tip at the corner of each eye—giving her a catlike appearance. She raved about taking an extra hour each morning to apply her makeup. She didn't leave the house without it.

I suspect she was in her late forties, even though the wear and tear of stress and unhappiness seemed to rob her of collagen. For a big woman, she wore a sunken, gaunt-like face. Her thinning blond hair, with gray tracing the edges, was usually tied back into a ponytail.

## Chapter 5: The Poor, the Rich, and What's Possible

She was one of the nicest people on the line—a ball of energy.

I called her "Miss Ethel." My strict, Christian upbringing required I address any adults as either "Mr." or "Miss" or "sir" or "ma'am."

Miss Ethel talked exhaustively about her seven kids and her husband, whom she described as a "lowdown dirty dog." She held nothing back from my young, impressionable ears. A smile rolled over her face when she mentioned her children. She never talked about them going to college. For her, a high school diploma was a huge accomplishment, something that had escaped her. She dreamed of her four sons taking a job in the plant alongside her, and she hoped her girls would find a nice man to take care of them, settle down, and get married.

Her dreams for her children were different from the vision Mom had instilled in us.

Like Mom's experience, poor was all Miss Ethel and her people had ever known, and neither Mom nor Ethel had finished high school when they were young.

Miss Ethel wanted what my mom sought—a better life for her kids. However, unlike Mom, she couldn't see beyond her own impoverished existence. Her mindset was fixed; you are who you are.

Can you relate to any of this? Your mindset is like a seed that has been planted in your brain. It grows and sprouts roots, soon taking control of your mind, and in many ways it can become your coping mechanism when you're questioned as to why you haven't changed or moved beyond your circumstances. I know the fear of the unknown is what leaves you stuck in your predicament. I know firsthand. I've watched people struggle, and even those with faith often succumb to fear—that powerful force that can keep you stuck in a certain mentality.

When poverty is all you've ever known for generations, with seemingly no way out, you tend to accept what is as your lot in life. Being financially poor can define who you are if you let it. It can create a story about who you are and who you'll never be. Visions of "a lot more money" is just "pie in sky"—a phrase I'd hear a lot in the plant.

Mr. Bobby Jo was a big man, probably pushing the age of sixty. He was pale with broad shoulders. One of his arms was more ink than skin. A large tattoo of a bald eagle covered his shoulder, and a menacing snake crawled up his arm toward the bird. Bobby Jo only finished the fourth grade. His daddy had pulled him and his brothers out of school to work and help feed the family. Mom worked three rows over, on the seamstress line, and she always kept a watchful eye on me and Mr. Bobby Jo. She didn't like the way he looked at me, and he was always offering to set me up with his son.

The plight of our destitute lives seemed to be the topic of conversation each day. The workers nearby, those who worked in the belly of the plant, often mumbled bitter words about never having enough to get by, or they spoke

## Chapter 5: The Poor, the Rich, and What's Possible

of their children or the gossip in the town.

Whenever politics came up, which was often, the workers all spewed the same rhetoric—rhetoric that made me cringe. They would tout their supposedly Christian and deeply conservative views. Their words became harsh and crude—mostly about "crooked rich folks." Jimmy Carter was the president at the time, and they would rail over the loud machinery, cussing almost daily about his policies. Mr. Bobbie Jo and his buddies were upset at Gerald Ford for losing to Carter, and they blamed Democrats for their financial ills and all that was wrong with our country. "Morally corrupt baby killers, abortion lovers," they'd fume. "Those crooked rich folks up in Washington don't care about us hicks down here. Did you see Carter pardoned the Vietnam War draft wimps? Good-for-nothin' draft dodgers, rich boys whose daddies protected them from serving," they'd rage. There was always someone else to blame for any problem.

Some days they'd wait in silence for my response, but I never participated. That was grown-up conversation. I never let on that I knew a lot about politics.

"We don't like cussin' 'round you, gal, we just hillbillies down here," Miss Ethel would say.

"You 'bout to go to college around dem proper folk," said Bobby Jo, snickering. "We ain't nothin' 'til they need our vote," someone else chimed in.

Even though we were all Christians, it was obvious to

me that we didn't share the same views on poverty. For one, Mom never blamed someone else for her lot in life. She took ownership of her mistakes and focused on trying to dig herself out of her financial hole. She never waited for the government to come rescue her children.

There seemed to be a mountain of misery in their lives. I did not understand the scope and depth of their anger. I felt that in knowing and loving God, there must be something to be grateful for. But each day, I was covered in stories of sadness and madness. Their lives seemed to be full of chaos, and they blamed the rich for their misery. It would have been easy for me to fall into this "victim mentality," but my job there was an opportunity to help Mom pay for my college education. It was just a stepping-stone to the greatness I hoped to achieve.

I'm only able to tell this story because I ignored the lie that I would never escape a life of poverty. Instead, I believed in myself and kept the fire inside me burning for a better life.

There were happy people at the plant, but they didn't work within earshot of me. When I would take my breaks, I'd walk by a few faces painted with expressions of joy. I do recall one day when they all perked up—there was a rumor of an upcoming ten-cent pay raise along with time off. Other than that, it was mostly depressing talk, especially for a teenager.

It was important that I focus on Mom's lesson that an education would plow my path to prosperity. I could not

## Chapter 5: The Poor, the Rich, and What's Possible

allow Bobby Jo and the others to color my judgment of the world.

While I didn't voice those views, they knew I saw the world differently.

"This girl is bent on goin' up the road and becoming one of them rich folks we see on TV," Bobbie Jo once said with a look of skepticism, shaking his head and darting his eyes toward Miss Ethel. She smiled and looked away.

"She wants to be an anchor," he said sarcastically. "What the hell is an *anchor*?" He stood silently staring at me, eyes perched above his glasses. "Ain't that somethin' you throw over a boat?"

I smiled nervously, unsure as to whether he was kidding. "I'm going to study journalism. I want to become a journalist, like Walter Cronkite, the news man you see on TV."

"That's for rich folk. We country bumpkins down here in the sticks don't need all that," he continued. Then a look of curiosity would creep over his face. "Who yo daddy?" he bluntly asked. Back then, your worth was measured by what your father did for a living. "How is yo momma gonna afford that high-cost schoolin' while workin' here?"

I realized they saw me as they saw themselves—stuck in poverty, with no way out.

By reading this, you might think I grew up around a backwoods clan of misfits—but those were my people.

They were good, hardworking, some wounded by a harsh life, at times misguided, but always well-intentioned.

Listening to the impoverished adult voices in that factory every day made me realize that many poor people tend to focus on what is not possible. I would later learn that the wealthy typically believe nothing is impossible.

## The Life of Prosperity

Two decades later, I was far from that world of poverty, getting a glimpse of the other extreme: wealth.

I boarded a private, chartered jet as an invited guest. I sat in a luxuriously comfortable leather seat with ample leg room, enveloped in unbelievable decadence. I'd traveled first class many times before, but this was an experience dreams were made of.

The friends who'd invited me, whom I'd met through a mutual friend at my television station, lived in a multimillion-dollar mansion and had live-in help, with daily chauffeurs.

I was greeted warmly by two pilots and a two-person crew.

"Miss Robinson, can I get you something to drink? A cocktail, perhaps? A glass of white wine?"

"Can you make me a cosmo?"

"Sure, whatever you desire, we've probably got it," she answered, smiling. She was eager to satisfy me.

## Chapter 5: The Poor, the Rich, and What's Possible

One major perk when flying on a private plane is that you get to decide what you want to eat: sushi, steak, gourmet pizza, fresh seafood, salad, pasta. I had preordered salmon and asparagus with a light salad and cheesecake for dessert. The service provided was that of a fine restaurant in the sky, complete with fancy dinnerware. The champagne was chilled and ready.

I glanced away from the large TV screens and out the window to the private hangar. *This is how the super rich live*, I realized. It was a far cry from my days of taking the Greyhound bus home from college to visit my family.

I was traveling with wealthy, staunchly private people—the kind of people who don't talk about their wealth, nor did they openly flaunt it. Unlike the workers in the shoe plant who openly voiced their disdain for wealthy people, there was never any talk here about contempt for the poor—at least not in my presence.

I marveled at the personalized pampering by the airline host who met each passenger's every need with a gracious smile.

When we touched down in Washington, DC, two long, slick, black, luxury sedans drove out onto the tarmac. Men in matching black suits, crisp white shirts, and black ties were standing next to two open car doors, waiting as if the US president would be exiting the plane.

My friends and I were escorted to the first car as security waved several other passengers into the next. Someone got our luggage for us, and we had already been checked into the hotel when we arrived. When the car pulled up to the curb, onlookers stared, wondering who had just arrived.

Our entourage of six was impeccably dressed. I wore a royal blue designer dress, black leather pumps, and matching bag.

Upon our arrival at the hotel, onlookers on the street stared as the bellmen and staff readied to retrieve our luggage and open the huge double doors to the luxury hotel. I was introduced to a different world, so different that it seemed I had landed on another plant. "Who are you? I recognize you," one doormen said. Smiling, I responded, "I'm Romona." Our security lightly touched me on the back to keep me moving forward. "You look like one of those movie stars . . ." His voice trailed off as I continued into the hotel.

Check-in was unlike anything I had ever experienced—there was none. "Follow me," the security guard instructed as he waved me past the check-in desk.

"We don't need to check in?" I inquired. "No, Miss Robinson, it's all been taken care of." Security had my room key in hand and was escorting me to my room as a bellman followed with my bags. No paperwork, no credit card exchange, no driver's license needed.

We were getting the royal treatment. *Wow*, I thought, *this is what it's like to be rich. Whatever your heart*

Chapter 5: The Poor, the Rich, and What's Possible

*desires, the answer is yes.*

It was a bewildering shift from a time when it seemed nothing was possible to me. I was now in a moment when everything was possible.

My "rich experience" gave rise to thoughts of my childhood that twisted their way deep into my soul. My mind churned back to my days as a "poor girl"—when Mom was always broke or close to broke, and whenever we wanted something, the answer was almost always no.

## The Power of Possibility

Like in 1976, when I wanted something big.

During my junior year in high school, I looked like a self-confessed bony, ugly duckling, but then I suddenly felt like maybe, just maybe, I was starting to blossom.

I had earth-tone skin; big brown eyes; and long, thick hair, with a noticeable beauty mark under one eye. My anatomy undertook on a transformation of its own. I was tall—all legs and breasts. My body didn't feel like my own. My hips, behind, and thighs seemed to pop and mutate outward overnight. The boys found that appealing, though; it was a body I was not yet comfortable in. I equated beauty with money, and since there was no money for trendy clothes, popular hair treatments, and cute accessories, I always felt awkward with my appearance.

As I slammed my locker shut and turned to rush to class, a six-foot-four tower of mocha perfection was moving like a leopard with grace toward me. His smile lit his youthful, unblemished face in the semi-dark hallway. Everything about him exuded confidence. I remember thinking God had been overly generous when He created this boy.

"Congratulations, Romona," said James Byrd, one of the school's top basketball stars.

"For what?" I asked, both curious and nervous.

"You've been voted Junior Basketball Queen," he informed me, looking pleased to break the news.

Stunned, I paused, giving my brain a chance to accept the impossible. I then shot back, "Are you serious? Why me?"

"'Cause you're nice, and we voted for you."

"Really? Me?" I asked again, thinking he must be mistaken.

The homecoming senior king and queen were chosen by the student body, but the rest of the court was handpicked by the school's athletes. Everyone knew the honor was reserved for popular girls with great school spirit and good GPAs. And it was a not-so-well-kept secret that you'd only get named to the queen's court if you were actually "courting" one of the players. I could not claim the latter, but I *was* a great student and nice to everyone.

To say I was shocked was an understatement. But I was very flattered.

## Chapter 5: The Poor, the Rich, and What's Possible

Back home after school, the excitement wore off quickly.

"No, Romona, no!" Mom raised her voice, her brows creased and her face tense. "I ain't got no money fo no formal dress."

"Please, Momma." I begged her not to buy my homecoming gown from Goodwill or the Salvation Army. "All the other girls will be wearing pretty new dresses their parents bought them."

"Wear one of yo church dresses. They pretty," she suggested.

"No, Momma, it has to be a floor-length gown," I pleaded.

"Well, we ain't got one of those. I can take you up there to Goodwill and see if we can find something for a dollar or two. If not, you tell them teachers you can't be no queen. Tell 'em yo momma ain't got no money fo no fancy dress."

Running from the living room, I dove in my bed face-first, asking God to help, to save me from embarrassment. I didn't want to relinquish my title, and for once my heart yearned to feel special, like I mattered, like I belonged. I wanted to be swept up in a moment I could only dream about—like the girls in the fairy tales whose parents were not money-deprived. For once, I wanted to look in the mirror and see that the reflection staring back at me was envied, the belle of the ball.

I refused to give up as Mom said no to a dress each day for a week.

Then something wonderful happened. The power of God intervened. I brought home a certificate showing that I had once again made the honor roll and had perfect attendance for the third year in a row.

Momma grabbed my certificate and pressed it to her face, beaming, almost laughing, like there was an explosion of pride in her brain.

"I've been thankin' upon some thangs."

I knew that was usually a great sign. It meant Momma had been praying to God, and He had provided her with wisdom for the situation.

"I'm gonna make you a gown." She smiled. Mom's skill as a shoe seamstress often came in handy. She had become a self-taught dressmaker years before—a talent buried by the demands of raising her kids. "We gonna go to the fabric stoh Saturday and pick you out a pattern, and I'm gonna make yo dress. It's gonna be real pretty, you watch," she said with a look of determination.

Dozens of silky, shiny, and sparkly fabrics smacked us in the face when we entered the store. Every time I'd inch toward material over a dollar a yard, Mom would motion for me to follow her. I knew exactly where we were going. It was where we always ended up when shopping—at the sales rack in the back: *DEEP DISCOUNTS. NO RETURNS*, the sign read.

## Chapter 5: The Poor, the Rich, and What's Possible

But before I could dive into the fabrics, she pulled me toward the patterns. "You say you want a straight-fitted dress with a light shawl. Let's look at these Simplicity and Butterick books and find you a dress."

There were so many possibilities. It was a daunting and dizzying task. But one caught my eye, and Mom loved it. We slid open the huge drawer, hoping and praying my pattern number and size was in stock. We were in luck. She purchased the Butterick pattern, size 6, for fifty-nine cents.

It was a collarless dress with a slightly lowered, round neckline. The fitted bodice ended just below the bust, giving a high-waisted appearance, and a straight, floor-length, fitted skirt skimmed the body. Draped over the gown was a separate sheer, chiffon scarf. The see-through fabric burst with floral colors of yellow, pinks, and greens that complemented the pink gown. The peekaboo scarf was made to slip over the dress and came to right below the waist.

I was nervous when I saw the pattern wasn't long enough to accommodate my height. "That ain't a problem," Mom said. "I'll just buy some extra material and lengthen it for you. Remind me we got to account for the heels you gonna wear."

I kept that pattern for decades.

When it was finished, my dress was a work of art. Mom fitted it perfectly to my body. In every spare hour after work, even though she was bone-tired, she labored over my gown. I watched her lay out the paper pattern onto the fabric. She'd stick pins in it, mark it, and cut it. On another day it was time for measuring and stitching. The next day, her face was moist and her eyes strained as she widened and lengthen, then more fitting, cutting, and sewing. Bent over her sewing machine, exhausted, she labored for more than a week as she fashioned a dress we both could be proud of.

Her backbreaking, finger-numbing job at the factory was too much some days. When she couldn't steady her sore fingers to thread the needle, I'd do it for her.

Mom could not cage her enthusiasm during my final fitting.

"Turn around," she instructed, laughing, proud of her masterpiece. I delighted her with several twirls. The lightweight, multicolored, silk-like chiffon fabric moved as my body did, flowing like a light summer breeze.

"You look beautiful," she said. It might have been the first time Momma ever called me that. She was excited, even giddy, childlike as she marveled at her stellar work, pleased she had made me happy. Momma's dress rivaled the store-bought ones.

There was a burst of organized chaos as my six sisters helped me get ready for the homecoming football game and the dance afterward, which would take place in the high school gym. Brenetta, Evonne, Varnessa, Melissa,

## Chapter 5: The Poor, the Rich, and What's Possible

Rena, and Serderia all crammed in my room, and I twisted and turned in the mirror so much my sisters cautioned I'd faint if I didn't stop. I loved how my shawl moved effortlessly in motion directed by each turn.

The huge, fluffy curls in my hair seemed to dance in harmony with every tilt and turn of my head. The pain of sleeping in giant rollers overnight had paid off.

"Wow, you look so pretty, like a movie star," one of them said.

"No, you look like Cinderella," someone else called out as I spun around.

Mom had become my fairy godmother. It took more than a magic wand, but what she birthed in me with that dress was a sense of pride. I felt like I measured up to my peers, and for once my poverty existence took a back seat.

As I got a final glimpse of my image in the mirror, I marveled at Mom's talent—$3.50 for six yards of fabric, 50 cents for my shawl, and 20 cents for thread.

The night continued as a dream. My name was announced onstage, and everyone applauded as I walked forward. Both my escort and my classmates said I looked pretty. But none of it matched the look on my mom's face or my feeling of pride and hope—that just maybe, anything was possible, even if we didn't have much money.

## The Mindset Switch

After my glamorous weekend of private jet travel, I was grateful for all I had achieved and all I had experienced. I remembered that hopeful young girl I had once been.

I also remembered lessons from a mom who taught me that prosperity was possible if I believed in the Lord and worked hard to achieve my goals.

I discovered on my journey that changing my mindset about my money and rethinking how I spent it was key to achieving my financial goals. I had to first start believing prosperity was possible and applying all that I had learned.

Each of us eventually come to a reckoning in our lives. We must choose who we are and who we want to be. It's easy to turn to a manual or a book from a financial guru teaching you how to invest or save. I believe all of us have the ability to prosper, but we have to get to the root of our money problems. If we don't kill the root, it will come back, and before we know it, we're back to careless spending habits.

If you don't take an oath to yourself that it is time for a new approach, that it is time to turn things around and handle your money differently, no book, manual, or Bible study can make you do it.

As a part of the have-nots, I grew up with people who wanted many of the same things rich people have: a great job, a loving family, maybe even kids. But the financial

## Chapter 5: The Poor, the Rich, and What's Possible

road they took to get there started many miles back.

Even so, many of them worked to change their destiny, not blaming others for their lot in life. Sure, life is unfair—I started out far behind other wealthy children—but the lessons I learned at home weren't taught in school. I hope someday financial lessons will become a part of the schools' curriculum. But parents encouraging and teaching their children the power of possibility and believing in themselves can change their circumstances even in the midst of struggles.

God's Word says change comes from within, not from change in our circumstances. In the book of Romans, the apostle Paul encourages believers to be transformed by renewing their minds. The Greek word for "transformed" is *metamorphosis*, meaning "to change." We all have the capacity to change and get on the road to financial independence.

God promises an abundant life. He doesn't want us to be trapped by a lack of money, living a barely-making-it life. Genesis 2:15 tells us that "the Lord God placed the man in the Garden of Eden as its gardener, to tend and care for it."

God wants us to renew our minds through prayer and search for different ways to work and pull ourselves out of a financial rut. He wants us to become good stewards by nurturing and growing our blessings and creating new things from the life He's given us.

Society has programmed us to believe that those who live beneath us are there because of their own free will. I read several articles on sustained poverty before writing this book, and many of them were heavy on statistics and not personal stories. Only the people living in poverty can tell you how they arrived in such dire straits and why it is so physically and mentally challenging to get ahead. My story is just one story, one person's lens into a life without a proper safety net, not nearly enough to tackle the complex problem. I know people might not know how to overcome poverty, fearing the unknown and believing they don't deserve more, but I've never heard anyone say, "I love being right here in this money pit." Poverty can corrode your soul, leaving you with a sense of contentment even in your discontent. I don't have all the answers, but I do know that when you are ready to try something new, to change old ways of thinking and become open to doing things a different way, positive change can happen. Many of the people in the plant I worked with were focused on what they didn't have: what was missing in their lives and what their circumstances were and would always be. *I was able to dig my way out by turning on that mindset switch and holding steadfast to God's promises of better days to come.*

*Chapter 5: The Poor, the Rich, and What's Possible*

> **REFLECTION POINT**
>
> We aren't born to doubt ourselves; we're a blank canvas as kids. It's when we start to absorb the noise and teachings around us that we take shape and develop into who we will become. Don't let doubts about financial success take root in your mind. People caused me to doubt myself; I didn't learn that at home. Peers told me if I went to a historically black college I'd never get a job. That was not true. I excelled to the top of my career.
>
> A makeup artist once told me the mole underneath my eye was distracting for TV and that I should consider having it removed, but it's part of who I am, I argued—her words made me doubt my appearance. Even when I was six years old and shared that I wanted to be on TV like Walter Cronkite, some teased that it was impossible for poor people like us, planting yet another seed of doubt—but my faith said that I could. And that is how you have to start to approach your situation saving your money.
>
> How have you pushed past the doubters?
> Are you on a path to saving?
> Write down your goal.

Let's talk about what's possible when you look at the deeper meaning behind why you might not be achieving financial success—and what you can do to turn things around and set yourself on a path to financial freedom.

I wrote this book for people who are open to taking an inward look at what might be causing their repeated money issues, specifically, why they are not saving more of it. For some of you, it may simply be due to hardship; like my mom, you may have to stretch your dollars and every dime counts. Like my mom, you may have to be strategic in how and where you cut back to find fifty or a hundred dollars a month you can save.

But for others, especially female entrepreneurs wearing the popular *BOSS* T-shirts—make sure you're making boss money moves. Get started on that that emergency fund and begin putting away money for retirement.

CHAPTER 6

# HOARDING MONEY AND RECKLESS SPENDING

I was in my early thirties, on my knees digging through my date's bottom bedroom dresser drawer. I was watching the door, listening for footsteps to make sure I was not caught. A voice inside whispered to me to stop what I was doing, that it was wrong. An even stronger voice fueled my curiosity to continue.

What I found was mind-blowing. Even today it's something I can't unsee.

Let me start at the beginning. It was a date I had fantasized about all week. I had met a young man who seemed to have it all—good looks, a radiant smile that lit up a room, and his being rich didn't hurt either. It was my first date with Shawn. He would not tell me where we were going—just to dress casually.

When he opened the door to greet me, I was surprised by his T-shirt and long shorts. "Wow, you look gorgeous, but you're way overdressed," he said. "Is that your definition of casual?"

"Well, yes," I shot back. I sported a fitted, multicolored silk blouse with jeans and designer pumps.

"I'd planned to take you to this spot I know for a picnic. You will be the best-dressed picnicker ever."

"A picnic sounds wonderful," I lied. I love a good time outside, as long as I'm not eaten up by bugs and it's not cold—but it was September in Cleveland, so it was a bit chilly. "You should have told me. You just said to dress casually. I'm wearing a dressy blouse, with chandelier earrings and high-heeled shoes. I won't be comfortable in this getup."

""I have some new T-shirts I was going to send to my sisters you could probably wear, if you want," he said. "They're in my dresser, in the second or third drawer."

So I found myself mindlessly rummaging through his bottom dresser drawer looking for a T-shirt to wear. As I flipped through the neatly folded pile, I saw dozens of men's XL or XL tees. Everything in the drawer was way too large to fit me. Shawn was nearly ten inches taller and a hundred pounds heavier than me.

He assured me I would find some new small and medium souvenir shirts, and he had instructed me to look in the second drawer. I found nothing I liked, so I frantically flung open the third drawer—which contained neatly organized socks. As he called from the living room asking

## Chapter 6: Hoarding Money and Reckless Spending

what was taking so long, I pulled out drawer number four. My eyes widened, my mouth fell open, and my body stiffened. The only reason for pausing was to catch my breath. Turning toward the bedroom door, I called back, "I'll be right there." I leaned back and then forward again to get an even closer look. "Five more minutes," I hollered, then covered my mouth with my hand, trying to give my mind a chance to comprehend what my eyes were witnessing. There must have been a million dollars or more in his bottom dresser drawer!

It was an unimaginable sight—a treasure trove of uncashed checks for $80,000, $100,000, $150,000!

"What on earth?" I muttered.

Suddenly the heat that enveloped my head from the shock masked the chill in the room. From my quick estimate, the checks must have been collected over a year's time. I dipped my hand in the pile. The crisp paper slipped in and out of my hands and between my fingers. Some were folded, weathered-looking, like they had been there for a while, and others felt new, hot off the printer. The checks were all addressed to Shawn. I was amazed at the riches I had stumbled upon. But I wasn't inside an armored truck or a bank fault; I was in my date's home.

*Is this some secret form of hoarding?* I wondered. Sliding the drawer shut, I was suddenly consumed with an avalanche of thoughts. I had almost forgotten what I was looking for.

*Should I broach the subject and ask why he keeps a stash of paper money in his bottom drawer? How will I explain why I was sifting through his personal belongings? Is it snooping if you stumble on it?* Technically, I hadn't been prying. How I could spin the story had me in a state of confusion. Would he believe me? Would this be our last date if I admitted I was overcome with curiosity and lingered awhile visiting too long with his riches?

I was a disciplined saver, so I could not remain quiet. Our relationship was new, but I had to know why his earnings were not at least in the basic safety of a bank. After all, he seemed intelligent, blessed with good looks and athletic talent.

My voice cracked with emotion as I broached the subject after I emerged from his bedroom. I could feel my heart racing. "I wasn't snooping, but while I was searching for a T-shirt, I saw you have a lot of uncashed checks in your bottom drawer. Why haven't you deposited your money?" I asked, my tone softening as I waited for his response.

He crossed his massive arms and leaned back in silence as I spoke. His long pause did not go unnoticed as he shifted uneasily in his intimidatingly large leather chair.

For a thoughtful moment, I gazed up at his face, searching for a sign of shame. There was none.

Instead, Shawn proceeded to tell me, with great force, how he cashed them when he needed large sums of money. "They're fine. I just throw them in there and use them

## Chapter 6: Hoarding Money and Reckless Spending

when I need them."

"But your money could be earning interest in the bank," I gently responded.

Shaking his head and tensing a bit, he emphatically disagreed. There was no sense of urgency to invest the money, he told me. Then: "I thought you wanted a T-shirt," he sternly said.

"I didn't find anything I liked. I'll just wear what I have on. I'm fine," I said.

I lied. I wasn't fine at all. I couldn't let it go. Pressing my lips together and speaking slowly, I tried to tread lightly because I was talking to a grown man, and I hardly knew about "his" livelihood. "Might I suggest you at least deposit the checks in an interest-bearing checking or savings account?" I opened my mouth to say more, but never got there.

"Let's go eat," he said, abruptly ending our conversation. I could feel from his quick, short responses that he was uncomfortable being told how to handle his money.

I dropped the subject so as to not spoil our afternoon.

Our relationship was short-lived. We were complete opposites. We didn't have much in common other than a shared physical attraction.

Shawn owned twelve cars for him and his family—bought with a signing bonus rumored to be upward of ten million dollars. He had two homes—one in Cleveland and a larger one in his hometown.

I was on a different path. I was continually making choices to lay the foundation for financial security.

It wasn't just money Shawn was careless with. He raved how about being a momma's boy, as his mother waited on his every whim. Imagine my shock when he asked after two dates if I would pick up his dry cleaning and a few groceries for him. His exceptional talent meant he had lived a life of entitlement. He had been coddled by his mom, catered to by his coaches, and pampered by educators. He wanted for nothing.

I, on the other hand, was the complete opposite. I was a farm girl from Missouri's heartland who had never known anything but hard work and sacrifice. When I did have a little left over, I saved it. Mom, my siblings, and I had scraped and clawed for everything we received.

Shawn had been told by his coaches that he and his family would never have money problems again in their lives. But the uncashed checks were only one sign of his money instability problems. There were hordes of aggressive female fans, baby mamas, and money leeches who hovered around him constantly.

Shawn was a man with no plan.

After we had been dating for only a few months, Shawn suffered a minor injury and was placed on injury reserve.

*STAR PLAYER SHAWN CARTER HAS BEEN PLACED ON INJURY RESERVE AFTER THE GAME.*

## Chapter 6: Hoarding Money and Reckless Spending

I sat stone-faced next to our sports director as he read the breaking news live on the air, pretending I was as surprised as the rest of the viewing audience.

Shawn had called to deliver the bad news a few hours earlier while I was at work. Later, back at his home, he hadn't gotten out the details on how long he'd be sidelined before his phone rang. I listened in utter disbelief as his sister said, "I'm sorry you got hurt," and then a few sentences later, asked, "When are you going to buy me the new Lexus you promised?" After he hung up, I said in astonishment, "You don't know how long you will be out, your money isn't guaranteed, but you're still going to buy more cars?"

As I started to observe his spending habits more closely, I realized he didn't have any—money simply flowed out endlessly and irresponsibly. It was clear his money mentality did not match mine. Prosperity had been dumped in his lap, and he was ill-equipped to handle it. He would buy rounds for everyone and at times boastfully pay for dinner for the entire party. The check totals were staggering—but he simply smiled, flashing more cash than I had ever seen at a dinner table. I'd overhear phone calls with other relatives who were asking for luxury cars, jewelry, and trips, and he'd simply say, "No problem." He was not interested in talking about tomorrow—he was only living for today.

Shaking my head in disbelief, I would ask, "What if you're cut from the team someday? You're coming off an injury—what if you get hurt again? What will you have to fall back on? What about starting a college fund for your kids?"

Nothing I suggested was viewed as an actionable step he needed to take. I recall he would always say, "I'm young, I'll do that later."

He freely admitted he hadn't been raised with anyone talking about the importance of saving money. His dad was a janitor, and his mom worked at the post office. He said they just "lived for today," trying to make ends meet and raise their kids.

It was the same money strategy he adopted later in life.

Shawn was not willing to allow his money to work for him through savings and investments; instead, his dollars were spent on pleasure in the moment.

I couldn't see a future of combining my finances with someone who was so careless with God's monetary blessings. He was a multimillionaire still trapped in a poor man's mindset.

## Stewarding God's Blessing

*You plant much but harvest little. You have scarcely enough to eat or drink and not enough clothes to keep you warm. Your income disappears, as though you were putting it into pockets filled with holes!*

—**Haggai 1:6** TLB

## Chapter 6: Hoarding Money and Reckless Spending

> *The wise man saves for the future, but the foolish man spends whatever he gets.*
> —**Proverbs 21:20** TLB

> *Wisdom is better when it's paired with money, especially if you get both while you're still living.*
> —**Ecclesiastes 7:11** MSG

I started to believe God was asking me to take a good, hard look at my life and rethink my actions and the results that would follow.

When we're young, we can be wooed by lots of money and good looks, and we don't give much attention to the future. But as we grow older and start thinking about settling down—maybe buying a house and saving for tomorrow—superficial things don't lead your decisions. I was now looking toward my future, so how a potential partner saved and spent his money was important. My FICO score was paramount as I started to contemplate buying my dream home. I had to ask myself some tough questions: Could I truly overlook the obvious? Could I see myself with a man who showed no interest in learning how to manage his money? A man who quickly started to treat me the way he treated his money—carelessly.

Shawn's attitude about money was troubling because, unlike most Americans, as a multimillionaire athlete, he had financial advisors at his disposal. The team provided free freshmen financial workshops, so the awareness of the pitfalls of financial scams had been provided when he entered the league. He could easily learn how to manage his money if he were open to fiscal advice. But some of us get set in our ways. It's comfortable. We aren't open to learning how to do things differently.

Shawn had all the money he could ever spend, but he lacked the wisdom necessary to protect it. The Scripture says that being wise with your money has many advantages.

Plagued by injuries, he would eventually succumb to them. After only a year into his new contract, he was cut from the team after sustaining a career-ending injury. His money was not guaranteed. He had possessed the financial power to live a life of prosperity, but he threw it all away. He lost most of the money his big contract had provided.

Looking back, I don't think Shawn put off saving because he didn't think it was important. I think he assumed there would be a lot more money down the road where that came from. That's a big risk in a risky line of work.

*Chapter 6: Hoarding Money and Reckless Spending*

> **REFLECTION POINT**
>
> How do you begin to tackle learned behaviors?
>
> Ask yourself whether you have always been susceptible to the voices in your head before you buy something. You know, the one that says, You should probably save most of that income tax refund. Or, maybe you should wait before you make that big purchase and save some of your money. The voice that pushes you to go ahead—you can afford those shoes or that furniture right now. You only live once—buy it, buy it!

I heard those voices many times—and I still do.

Rick Kahler, a financial planner and therapist, is a cofounder of the Financial Therapy Association. He and a group of researchers studied the psychological and emotional aspects of money. What they found is that 90 percent of financial decisions are made emotionally.

So, you see, it is possible to detach from the emotional and mind-driving forces that convince you to overspend. We all want to save more money, right? We tell ourselves we'll start saving once we get to a specific age, get a raise, or when our grown kids move out of the house.

But, in reality, you'll only start putting away money when you develop healthy money habits and your financial future becomes more important than your current wants.

Part of resetting your mindset is to recognize the trap. That soothing, kind enemy's voice will tell you not to delay gratification. Tomorrow can wait; live for today.

His whispers continue even when the voice of reason is reminding you why it's not a good idea right now.

Don't fall for it. Your thoughts will always be the beginning of an action when shopping. Many times, our goal to save isn't a big enough priority to delay the purchase of that new smartphone, sofa, or flat-screen TV. So, we spend our dollars away—or worse, we go into debt to fuel our desires to have more.

It is not easy to flip that mindset switch. Your emotions and thoughts are powerful. They dictate your moves 24/7—telling you when it's time to eat, sleep, work, or play.

When you make something a priority, you will invest in it. Whether that's your money, your job, your boyfriend, or losing weight, you'll find a way to make it happen.

## The Mindset Switch

Here's how I did it.

1. Take control of your money and do not allow it to control you.
2. Uncover your money trauma, and in doing so find the deeper meaning to your careless spending and saving habits.
3. Push yourself to do the head work and heart work required to attain financial freedom.
4. Don't settle for safe and convince yourself that you don't deserve more. Determine a formula that works for you.

CHAPTER 7

# EXCESS DOES NOT EQUAL SUCCESS

There was a time when I was dead broke—not just when I was a child, but as an adult, too. It was 1987, when I was a young anchor and reporter in Charleston, South Carolina.

I will never forget my twenty-seventh birthday. As I lay face-planted in my bed, with swollen, red eyes and trickling tears like scattered showers drenching my pillow, I cried out to God, asking, *Why have You allowed this?* My heart felt hollow. A deep sadness had taken hold. My brain was drained of critical thinking; I almost felt zombie-like. I had never been fired before, and I was shell-shocked it had happened. Even more, I couldn't believe how I'd been caught without a safety net.

It was one of the most desperate and depression-filled times of my life. It is astonishing the pain, embarrassment, and crushing anxiety a lack of money can cause. I was a college-educated journalist who had been taught better—but all of Mom's lessons had become a blur as I enjoyed the good life as an up-and-coming anchorwoman, including Mom's biggest piece of advice: "Save yo money for hard times." In my first job in Jefferson City, Missouri, three years before, I didn't save a penny. Honestly, saving was not a high priority after I'd graduated from college. I got an expensive two-bedroom apartment (in the hottest new property), then dressed it to the max with everything my money and credit cards could buy. I bought things for others, before saving for myself. I was young, and like so many others, I thought saving could wait.

I was shell-shocked, fired suddenly, and eventually forced to move in with my longtime boyfriend when my money ran out. He provided a roof over my head but no financial support on his tight budget.

I wrote in detail about this time in my earlier memoir, but I didn't elaborate on how I survived for four months without any help. Honestly, I was embarrassed to write about it—to tell just how low I had sunk.

Is any of this resonating with you? Do you remember a time when you yourself were shell-shocked by a huge money scare? You may have lost a job without notice and had no backup plan. Maybe you or a parent became suddenly ill, and your finances took a huge hit. Perhaps, because of alcohol or gambling vices, you lost all your money. Maybe you were forced into bankruptcy and embarrassed by how far you had fallen. I get it.

## Chapter 7: Excess Does Not Equal Success

Within a few weeks after losing my television job, my savings were gone, and the bills started to pile up. In the eighteen months I had worked in South Carolina, I had saved a couple hundred dollars, not nearly what I needed to have in an emergency fund. I received no severance package. I couldn't pay my rent, my car payment, my heating and cooling bills.

I hadn't been living above my means. I just spent every cent I earned. I'd made about $25,000 a year—a little better than the $18,500 the average American worker brought home at that time.

Looking back, I saw I made common mistakes. My new job paid $10,000 more than what I had previously made. Excited, I dumped my used 1982 Mustang II. I put $2,000 down on a brand-new Lincoln Mercury, plus with my trade-in, I could bring my car payment down to $400 a month. I splurged on new furniture, took lavish outings to nearby Hilton Head Island, updated my work wardrobe, and made endless, costly flights home to Missouri and visits to see my boyfriend in Washington, DC. I had turned my back on my sensible upbringing and the Bible's money principles of which I had been fed a heavy diet as a child. I wanted what I wanted—and I wanted it now.

After my termination, I was forced to visit an old friend. I hadn't seen him since college. His name? Ramen noodles. Thank goodness they were still cheap and delicious—you could still buy a package for less than a dollar, even cheaper in bulk. I ate them morning, noon, and night. My good ol' college buddy that had gotten me through the lean years was once again saving me from complete starvation. The yellow, stringy delight with flavorful seasoning packets had an addictive, satisfying taste. Some days, to prolong the meal, I slowly caught a few strands with my fork, twirled it around, and talked to myself, convincing myself it was the most delicious food ever and that it would sustain me. Other times, I'd wolf it down, seemingly without chewing, like it was my last meal. The hunger pangs could be so intense they created a gnawing, growling stomach that felt hollow inside. I found myself always evenly spacing out breakfast, lunch, and dinner, watching the clock and trying to rush evening time. I was in a state of delirium. Not only was my mind wasting away, but so was my body. I was the thinnest I'd ever been.

It never crossed my mind to call my mom and ask for help; after all, she still had three children at home to raise on her salary. And what would I look like, a college graduate and out-of-work journalist asking my struggling mom to help?

When you're hungry, you find money in unlikely places—change in between and underneath the driver's seat of your car, five-dollar bills in old purses, coats, and pant pockets, even in the crease of your sofa and chairs. I found loot everywhere—just like back in the days of the money hunts Evonne and I went on.

It was a dark and lonely time, and it was humiliating

## Chapter 7: Excess Does Not Equal Success

when the debt collectors start to call. They were like pit bulls, ferocious when it came to trying to recoup money for their clients. Thinking back, I can laugh at the creative ways I'd avoid them.

Several months in radio right out of college had helped me master changing the tone of my voice. My voice-over commercial work for different brands had called for a certain cadence. I adopted three alter egos to dodge their calls: I was a sweet old lady, a high-pitched receptionist, and a drill sergeant.

*Sweet old lady:* "Yello . . ." I'd pause, purposely sounding out the *y*, channeling my grandma. "Romona who?" I'd be slow to speak, sounding confused. "Hun, what you say now? Did you say *Corona*? Is that what you said . . . I'm uh, I'm sorry, baby, I don't have any Corona here. I recon you done dialed the wrong number."

*The receptionist*: "This is Miss Weaver, how can I help you?" I would ask in a strong, authoritative, professional voice.

"I'm looking for a Romona Robinson, is she home?" asked the caller.

"We have no one who works here by that name . . . You must have the wrong number." I never gave the creditor a chance to speak and quickly hung up.

*Drill sergeant:* In a lower baritone imitation with a no-nonsense delivery, I'd say, "Yeah? Who's calling?"

"Is Romona Robinson home?" the caller would ask.

"Nobody by that name lives here. No need to call here anymore, right?" That alter ego was the toughest, because I had to be stern and abrasive, which was not part of my personality.

I was not proud of my devious actions, but when you're out of work, stressed out, and with no way to pay a creditor, their calls can be daunting and degrading.

Trying to reassure bill collectors you'd pay when you got a job fell on deaf ears. They had a job to do—retrieve a company's money—and they didn't care about your personal situation.

This was a huge fall from grace that hit me like a ton of bricks. With no savings and no backup plan, I went from being a young, aggressive reporter who, some said, would shoot to stardom, to down and out and depressed. The fear of losing it all was mentally and emotionally crippling. The truth is, my faith wasn't as strong then, and I was reduced to a pile of teary-eyed chaos in my head. I cried a lot, and Satan visited often, confirming my negative thoughts.

After two months of unsuccessfully searching for a television job, I heard from my apartment manager. He politely told me it was time for me to move; he could no longer allow me to live there rent free. He had been overly generous. His glassy eyeballs, bright red cheeks, and slow delivery told me how hard it was for him to ask me to leave. I had no other choice. I reluctantly moved in with my boyfriend-turned-fiancé in DC. If you have

## Chapter 7: Excess Does Not Equal Success

read *A Dirt Road to Somewhere,* you know our road to marriage did not work out. And neither did the job I took as a Lancome cosmetics sales associate at Hecht's, a department store in nearby Maryland, partly because my coworkers perceived me as a woman of privilege and status and therefore viewed me as uptight, arrogant, and entitled. They didn't know I didn't have a dime to my name.

"I hear you're a bigtime news anchor," one of them said a few days after I'd started the job. "Is that where you got those fancy suits you parade around in?" she asked sarcastically. "Why is someone like you working at a department store anyway?" You've met the type, those who love to poke the bear when it is hibernating and has lost its fight.

I grew silent, looking her way with a gentle smile. My wardrobe consisted of mostly tailored, figure-flattering skirt suits and dresses with matching pumps—leftovers from my years in television. I'd never made enough for designer outfits, but I loved looking professional with a kick of elegance. I was tall and thin as a rail from all those ramen noodles I was living on.

The comments didn't stop the whole time I worked there. "You've got a fancy college degree in television, and you're slapping makeup on these common folk?"

With my TV career seemingly over, my relationship with my boyfriend falling apart, and the constant taunting at work, I started to sink into a mild depression. My road to prosperity had taken a wrong turn, and I was lost. Maybe you can relate to this suffering when you're working at a job you hate, but you need it because you have responsibilities and bills to pay. You have a lot of time to reflect about things you could have and should have done differently. For me, I was taught to use my common sense—I knew the consequences if I was ever fired with no savings. I just didn't think it would happen to me.

It was daily Scripture reading and increasing faith that started to fuel me. I drew on the lessons from my childhood—the knowledge that God would never leave me nor forsake me. That's where I found my safe haven: in the Word of God.

> *I called to the LORD, who is worthy of praise,*
> *and I have been saved from my enemies.*
> **—Psalm 18:3 NIV**

During this time, I first started to make the correlation between being confident in who I was or allowing what people thought of me to pull my mental purse strings.

When you're able to find "your" worth in Jesus, not in how much money you do or don't have, you no longer feel you have to live up to the idea of someone else's perceived success—and it is powerful. My faith in the Lord told me I would see better days ahead.

> *Wealthy people invest first and spend what's*

*Chapter 7: Excess Does Not Equal Success*

*left; poor people spend first and may save what's left.*

—**Anonymous**

## Starting Fresh

Nearly nine months passed before I landed a coveted television job in Cleveland. I got my second chance—a chance to get it right and chart a new course of financial responsibility. I knew what I would do within the first year: pay off all my debt. I owed $15,000 to creditors and in student loan debt. I didn't make big money purchases as soon as I got to town. Instead, I hunkered down in a small but nice apartment below my means and continued to drive my used Lincoln Mercury Thunderbird. I needed the bulk of my paycheck to pay back defaulted loans.

When I got my first paycheck, it was tempting to run out and spend, to buy something expensive because I hadn't been able to do so for nearly a year—but I didn't. I had called all my creditors when I was fired and vowed that as soon as I got a job, I would pay off my debt. I was true to my word and my God.

> *The wicked borrow and do not repay, but the righteous give generously.*
> —**Psalm 37:21** NIV

I lived by my beliefs and the Bible. God's Word talks a

great deal about debt. God does not look kindly on people who cheat and steal. It's also how I was raised. If you borrow money, pay it back.

The Bible isn't silent about debt. There were obviously no credit cards, mortgages, or car loans in Jesus' time, but lending and borrowing were still part of the economic landscape. The Bible doesn't strictly prohibit incurring debt, but it does characterize debt as a form of bondage.

> *The rich rule over the poor, and the borrower is slave to the lender.*
> **—Proverbs 22:7** NIV

My life changed dramatically once I moved to Cleveland. Happiness returned to my soul. I had been hired as a primary evening news anchor at WUAB-TV, an independent television station. I was the first black woman named in that role in Cleveland, but I was not rich. I only made fifty grand my first year. The truth is, though, I would have taken half that amount just to get back in the business.

Money wasn't the only perk. I had position and power. Not only would I make history, but I had the power to help decide what stories we did and didn't cover.

It's tempting when you first get a new job that bumps your salary to spend some and spend it fast. Suddenly your needs take a back seat to the wants, and you can get a case of amnesia—forgetting all the money lessons you were taught, all the promises you made to God if He

## Chapter 7: Excess Does Not Equal Success

would just rescue you. It didn't happen to me—at least not at first.

We inherit what we know about money mostly from our parents. When you grow up in a household that scrapes to get by, you often try to make up for the childhood you didn't have, and you want extravagance for yourself and your children. But that gratification can be short-lived, especially if you have a life-altering emergency in your life—like the loss of a job or a severe disability or illness.

When I thought about that time when I lost my job in Charleston, I used to beat myself up mentally. *How could you not have an emergency fund? Why were you not at least invested in the the 401(k)s offered at your last two jobs? Why didn't you retain a lawyer and fight for a severance package when you were let go?* You don't know what you don't know.

My mother had taught me so many faithful financial lessons—mostly about putting my money in the bank. Most people are trained to put away money away in a savings accounts—not investing it. Our parents taught us only as much as they knew.

Still, I was embarrassed that I could have allowed myself to be in that position.

I was determined to create healthy financial habits moving forward. I never wanted to feel that kind of desperation again, having no control over tomorrow, not knowing if or how long I'd have a roof over my head, scraping to get by, fearing creditors would make good on their promises and have me arrested if I didn't pay up.

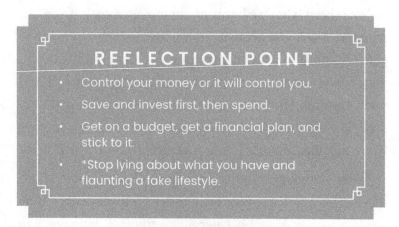

> **REFLECTION POINT**
> - Control your money or it will control you.
> - Save and invest first, then spend.
> - Get on a budget, get a financial plan, and stick to it.
> - *Stop lying about what you have and flaunting a fake lifestyle.

## Living for Now

I've met and talked to a lot of people about money, and it's shocking how many of them disregard the basic financial lessons they know in favor of having what they want right now.

A coworker once called me over to his desk to show me the expensive wine he was ordering from Italy for his new female friend.

"That's nearly three hundred dollars!" I exclaimed.

"I know! Won't she be impressed?" he whispered, blushing.

"You've only been dating for a week," I said. "Aren't you the same man who told me over and over again that you don't save your money?" He'd actually told me that

## Chapter 7: Excess Does Not Equal Success

his net worth was zero and that he wasn't saving for retirement, even though the company offered matching 401(k) contributions.

"I know, I know, I'm nearing forty, and I should be saving, but I just love buying expensive things. I don't know why."

"You make a six-figure salary, and you have no savings. What if something happened? What if you lost your job or became ill? You need a plan!"

"I know . . . You're right, Romona, but you only live once, and I want to enjoy all that my salary affords me. I live a great life."

It's tough for this man to break the debilitating patterns that keep him from having a money plan, because he can't see the destructive journey he is on and he isn't willing to listen. He is fixated on the here and now—and that is never a recipe for financial success. He had allowed society to lure him into a behavior pattern that convinces us we must buy everything we can, that excess equals success. When I lost my job, I soon realized that was a lie. All that excessive spending equals debt.

It's a conversation I've had over and over with people of all income levels. Ideas like retirement and financial literacy didn't light up their brains, even those who admitted they were struggling. They grew quiet when I talked about delayed gratification.

Nearly forty million households have no retirement

savings at all, according to the National Institute on Retirement Security. I was not surprised in my interviews with millennials with good-paying jobs, to find that none had a six-month emergency fund. They admitted shallow behavior, telling me that what society says about beauty and wealth impacts their spending, including the latest hairstyles, clothing, cars, and entertainment.

We used to call this behavior "keeping up with the Joneses," but now I know the Joneses were probably broke too.

When you are bombarded with constant advertising, it can make you feel inadequate, unsatisfied with your current situation. We have been programmed to believe that vanity and our possessions are what it takes to truly be happy instead of being honest and kind. We are influenced to hoard rather than to help.

I've learned one of the biggest misconceptions people have about money is that they don't need to address their feelings about it. The relationship you have with your dollars is tied to your deeply held beliefs and spending attitudes, and we all should reexamine these from time to time. Those habits can block your savings path and ultimately prevent you from reaching your financial destiny.

And contrary to popular belief, it's not only some low-income and middle-income earners who blow through their paychecks each month. Many high-income earners also live above their means. Studies show that at least a

## Chapter 7: Excess Does Not Equal Success

quarter of households making $150,000 and above live from paycheck to paycheck.

Most people would rather "look rich" than do the work necessary to build wealth. They spend their entire paychecks to maintain their lifestyles.

Has this ever been true of you?

When I really started to become a television success, at first, I got caught up in the flashy game. I once bought an expensive three-piece Louis Vuitton luggage set on a whim. I wanted it simply because it was "in." Everyone who was anyone was sporting that luggage set, and I wanted to show I was one of the cool kids too. It was a behavior that was not me, but I succumbed to the societal pressure to appear perfect.

With everything I had been taught about saving money, I was beginning to morph into someone I didn't even recognize.

As soon as I earned it, all my money went right back out the door to support the good times. And yet I had an emergency fund and had started to invest.

Thank goodness my flashy stage was short-lived, and that good sense my mom talked about kicked in when the Louis Vuitton luggage came off the conveyor belt at the airport with a huge oil spot and scuff marks after only one use.

Devin, a thirty-year-old who agreed to talk to me, came from nothing as I did, and he reluctantly confided that he was broke. He was also honest about why. "I got a degree," he said. "But I got tired of working two jobs as a mortgage lender and an Uber driver every day and not winning. I was beating myself up because I couldn't keep pace financially with my friends. I wanted to be sleek and flashy, to be seen and heard in a world that virtually ignores poor people. Where I grew up, excess equaled success, so I had to show my people I had made it So, I went credit-card crazy. I had about seven of them. I'm trying to do better now. I've paid off four of the cards. I plan to climb out of this."

Shelby, age twenty-six, the youngest of the people I interviewed, actually called me saying she had come into a $20,000 inheritance and wanted to know about where she might invest it. She quickly said, "I want to go to Florida and maybe take a trip to Las Vegas, too." I suggested she could do both—as long as she saved at least seventeen or eighteen thousand dollars of the money. I believe in fun money and not totally restricting yourself. As a young person, you can become unhappy, feeling like life is passing you by if you don't have a little fun money to spend. After a short conversation, she said, "I think I want to put it in a savings account." I quickly cautioned against that, citing easy access to her cash can be too tempting. I suggested she put it into an investment account where she couldn't touch it until she was fifty-nine, or suffer a penalty. She was done and said, "I'll call you back."

Growing wealth means you have to be ready and

## Chapter 7: Excess Does Not Equal Success

willing to change how you've always done things. When you allow yourself to believe the ideas that say: *I will always be restricted*; *I'm poor, and there are no signs I will fulfill my financial dreams*; *it's important to have fun now, because I could be hit by a car at twenty-two*—I also believe you could outlive your savings and end up at the mercy of the state at seventy-two.

These stories show what financial experts describe as wanting to avoid any short-term money discomfort—they only seek the pleasure of what it affords now. Unfortunately, that clashes with what they care about in the long term, what's important to them, what gives them purpose, what gives them true meaning in their lives. Not socking away a portion of a huge salary is obviously not the way to gain financial freedom later in life.

> **REFLECTION POINT**
>
> Maybe you see yourself in some of these stories. The only way to have a worry-free financial life is to become a different person, to cut the excess spending out of your life.
>
> And, like me, if you find yourself out of a job suddenly with no warning:
>
> - Don't become bitter after being fired—get better.
> - Get better at recognizing potential problems, staying ahead of unforeseen challenges, and making connections.
> - Build the courage to stand up to life's challenges.
> - Spend twenty-four hours if you need it to cry it out, but then get up the next day and activate the superpower in you.
> - Draw on your inner strength, the motor that kicks in and helps you stand up to fear and unfairness.

## Wisdom on Spending

I didn't write this book to sell a prosperity gospel. Instead, this is a candid and intimate look at what worked for me and the people I interviewed who were willing to share their stories. However, a huge part of my life is my faith and the wisdom that comes from it.

Scripture spells it out quite simply: It is better to spend

## Chapter 7: Excess Does Not Equal Success

less than you earn and it is foolish not to save—no matter how much you're making. Many of us also covet things, and we are willing to go into deep debt to have them.

The Bible says, "The wise store up choice food and olive oil, but fools gulp theirs down" (Proverbs 21:20 NIV).

When we are young, we are given all kinds of wise advice about right and wrong, relationships, education, getting a job, and buying a home. But no one tells us about being wise with our money in our later years. Most kids don't get serious talks about financial planning and pitfalls to avoid the mental money traps that can derail your plans for financial independence.

> *But those who desire to be rich fall into temptation, into a snare, into many senseless and harmful desires that plunge people into ruin and destruction. For the love of money is a root of all kinds of evils. It is through this craving that some have wandered away from the faith and pierced themselves with many pangs.*
>
> **—1 Timothy 6:9–10** ESV

Unfortunately, I've known people struggling to have a long-term financial mindset—from all socioeconomic backgrounds. Many people would rather "look rich" than do the work to build wealth. They spend their entire paycheck to maintain a lifestyle that matches their peers.

We try to conform to what society says we should be,

but the Bible says, "Do not continue to conform to the pattern of this world" (Romans 12:2 EHV).

In *The Living Bible,* this verse reads: "Don't copy the behavior and customs of this world, but be a new and different person with a fresh newness in all you do and think. Then you will learn from your own experience how his ways will really satisfy you."

I needed to realize my worth was not found in trying to impress people by the things I have; it was in how I felt about me. Once you find "your" worthiness, you will no longer feel you have to live up to someone else's perceived success—and this is powerful. No matter how much experience you have, how many degrees you achieve, or how popular you are—there will always be someone smarter, prettier, and more successful than you.

There's nothing wrong with spending money as long as it's not detrimental to yourself and your long-term goals. Stop feeling the need to prove something to other people by coveting materialistic items and going into debt to acquire them.

People in Cleveland reading this who watched me dressed to the nines for decades on television might think, *How hypocritical—she wore beautiful clothing each night,* but you'd be surprised what I paid for many of my suits and dresses. Yes, I had designer clothes because I could afford them, but by far, most of my wardrobe came from bargain shopping. I refused to conform to the idea that I needed designer tags to keep up with others. I did

## Chapter 7: Excess Does Not Equal Success

not care if someone said, "I saw that at TJ Maxx," or "I got the same $89 dress from Dillard's." So what? The confidence in knowing I was okay with me prevented foolish spending.

Instagram is loaded with pictures of young people drenched in designer wear, others flashing the latest gadgets—iPhones, expensive headphones. Some are driving fancy cars they've financed for seven years to make the payments. Yet, they are consistently broke. Many want expensive toys now. Why save for it when you can just charge it right now?

It's not easy—I know. Sometimes life's challenges just seem impossible to overcome. You suffer financial troubles everywhere you turn, and just when you think you're about to have a breakthrough—something else goes wrong.

Maybe you're dealing with family financial issues or a divorce. Your spouse or partner is arguing over money, or you've received an unexpected medical bill. You want to buy a new car or take that fancy trip. Yet you suffer setback after setback. It's enough to make you believe you're never going to win at anything. You start to feel that maybe God has forgotten about you. Or, as I like to say, "Maybe He's punishing me for something I did in another life?" My husband chuckles at that one every time.

But God doesn't care about the material things you want or possess.

Look at what He said to Samuel: "Don't judge by a man's face or height, for this is not the one. I don't make decisions the way you do! Men judge by outward appearance, but I look at a man's thoughts and intentions" (1 Samuel 16:7 TLB).

A transformation took place took place when I made the correlation between being confident in who I am on the inside and not my outward appearance and my collection of things. I no longer allow what people think of me to pull my mental purse strings (which ultimately means I stand in my truth and say, "This is what's true about me").

So, while we're working to accumulate a bunch of things, God is more interested in our heart and how we use His many blessings. Are you coveting or hoarding money, helping the needy, and giving of your time? Are you living out His purpose for your life?

Many millennials like Devin admit they're more focused on paying for "experiences" than saving for their future. I've witnessed how some treat their financial health, how they treat their finances—they think saving can wait because they're still young.

There's nothing wrong with wanting to be young and fabulous—as long as you're socking away some of that money for your future.

Four out of five older millennials nearing forty admitted to me they are living fabulous lives—and are broke. They crave expensive experiences, driving tricked-out dream

## Chapter 7: Excess Does Not Equal Success

cars like Lexuses, Benzes, or Range Rovers, and saving money is quite low on their list of priorities.

It is no surprise why they are all nearly broke. All of them say they were never taught specific money lessons. Sure, they heard the standard "get an education so you can get a job" speech, but they learned nothing about investing and preparing for their financial futures.

All of them know it is important to save and earn more than you spend, but for many, saving can wait. They are young and want to have fun. So many fall into the trap of trying to flaunt a certain lifestyle, so people will think they're rich, when, in reality, they're broke—running up their credit cards. They are not ready to accept that *they are enough*, no matter what the world says about being rich.

They've been programmed to view money by what they see on TV and social media. Their friends and peers are living seemingly incredible lives, and they want it too. Don't fall into the trap of the pressure to look perfect. You'll end up faking a life of perfection, or worse, becoming dependent on someone else, if not becoming a burdeon on your parents or children.

Appearances can be deceiving. A well-known rapper was once photographed in front of a private jet he was pretending to take to a destination, only to be captured in a picture by a fellow passenger actually flying commercial at the same time.

*The naive believes everything, but the sensible man considers his steps.*

— **Proverbs 14:15** NASB

I get it. In one year, my salary doubled. I started to hang out with people who were adventurous and who wanted to live large—spending New Year's Eve in New York City or purchasing ringside seats at a Tyson fight in Vegas. Taking trips on a whim to exotic places, impulsive Rolex and Chanel purchases, dining at four-star restaurants and staying at five-star hotels. I had developed an interest in the finer things in life—a far cry from the poverty in which I grew up.

With everything I had been taught about saving money, though, I was beginning to morph into someone I didn't recognize.

As soon as I earned it, it all went right back out the door to support the good times. Even though I had an emergency fund and had started to invest, I only had enough to live on for four or five months without withdrawing from my 401(k) if there was another unexpected emergency. So, I let myself become a little vulnerable, and I knew I needed to do better—and I did over time.

I was in my late thirties when I finally became totally comfortable with who I am and whose I am. That was the result of spending the decade prior rededicating my life to God. I joined a great church and started doing what I did as a child: reading my Bible. And more than that, I started

## Chapter 7: Excess Does Not Equal Success

believing in the Word. My talks with myself and with God helped me understand that I didn't need to impress other people with the things I possessed. I was good enough in His eyes. Today, I'm more impressed with a good FICO score, some savings, and a financial plan. I want you to remember what I finally got, that every time you thoughtlessly overspend, your spending brings insecurity while saving brings security.

My money trail has not been perfect. I have made a lot of mistakes. Thankfully, I learned young that you have to change your beliefs about you first, and then you'll become more responsible with your dollars.

(You'll find great information at a site called *Money Smart for Young People* at fdic.gov. If you're over forty, I like *Money Smart for Adults* at fdic.gov.)

If you're struggling while reading this, stop saying, "Woe is me . . . I have so little I've gotta charge it to buy it and fit in." Stop the negative talk. You've already convinced yourself it's not even worth taking a look at where you might save. Baby steps are okay. Just get started. Change your thinking about yourself, about your money, and about your future.

## REFLECTION POINT

Money problems can make you feel small. They can take away the little dignity you have left—unless you constantly feed yourself words of wisdom about being good enough, smart enough, and brave enough to overcome your circumstances. By now, your mindset transformation is complete. Hopefully, you are motivated to get on the path of sustained saving.

This chapter has stressed how a transformation can take place in your life when you're able to find your worth in Jesus, and not in how much money you do or don't have—and it is powerful.

I shared one of the most desperate and depression-filled times of my life when I was broke and had no place to live. My hope is that you will be able to adopt a new mindset rooted not in what the world says about wealth and worthiness, but in what God says. If we believe we are good enough in God's eyes, the opinion of others is not important.

- Don't start to live under a spell cast by society and become a fake version of yourself.

- Break the cycle. We have become seduced by what we see, and we want bigger and better than our peers.

- Even with your Louboutin red-bottom shoes, those insecurities that you haven't worked on still exist.

CHAPTER 8

# FRIENDS AND FINANCIAL FOOLISHNESS

I started outlining my book several months before anyone knew there would be a global pandemic. The economic tailspin the virus threw us into affirmed why my book is needed now. People's finances were exposed. Recent data shows that at the beginning of 2020, the average American family didn't even have $400 in an emergency fund and were ill-equipped to handle an unexpected job loss—let alone a prolonged economic catastrophe.

As I put the finishing touches on the manuscript before, during, and now, still coming out of the pandemic, the economy has been a roller coaster. Although jobs are plentiful, inflation is at its highest level in decades, and so are interest rates, the stock market is rocky, and experts say savings are up over pre-pandemic levels, but people are still spending. They also predict people's lack of saving attitudes will return as soon as we weather the storm.

Sometimes the struggle to save comes not from society, but from your own friends and peers—even your family members. You may be trying to live financially smart, putting away money for your retirement, but the lure to "keep up with the Joneses" can be tempting.

> *Everyone wants to ride with you in the limo, but what you want is someone who will take the bus with you when the limo breaks down.*
> **—Oprah Winfrey**

Money can have a huge impact on friendships. I myself have not been immune from snobbish foolishness.

In 1995, I was happy with where my path and purpose was taking me. I was becoming a successful young news anchor. One night, a new friend and I were headed to the club. I offered to drive us there in my Ford Explorer.

"We cannot pull up to the club in a Ford," she said. "We'll take my Porsche." She beamed with pride and a sense of accomplishment.

She was consumed with appearances, wanting to give the impression she was rich. She was a thirty-two-year-old Realtor, but she acted more like an heiress—with a fancy car and designer clothes. Our friendship was short-lived, so I never saw how she actually lived.

I could have been hurt by her shallow remarks, had I not grown up around people with so little but who focused on being grateful for what they had. When you've floated

## Chapter 8: Friends and Financial Foolishness

between poverty and achieving the material riches life has to offer, you become either grateful and share your abundance or you become selfish and hoard your wealth.

I had no money concerns at the time.

I was living a modest lifestyle, working as an up-and-coming television anchor in Cleveland. I had the means to afford a luxury car, designer dresses and shoes, and exotic vacations taken on a whim.

Instead, I brown-bagged it and skipped the fancy restaurants and clubs with colleagues each night.

I wasn't broke, but in addition to carving out a nice nest egg for my future, I also wanted to build a custom home.

In Luke 14:28 Jesus said, "Suppose one of you wants to build a tower. Won't you first sit down and estimate the cost to see if you have enough money to complete it?" (NIV).

After considering the cost of my new home, I came up with a strict two-year savings plan. A 20 percent down payment was a must. I was determined not to pay PMI (the mortgage insurance you pay when you put less than 20 percent down). I was also socking away extra funds to furnish the home and all the other financial commitments that come with home ownership.

I was teased relentlessly by a few people who saw my rides: my Explorer SUV for Cleveland's harsh winters and my Ford Taurus sedan.

"How much are they paying you, Romona?" a coworker asked with a smirk. "Surely you could afford a luxury car, an anchor of your stature."

Each time I explained that I was saving to build a home, but people still judged me. The jokes were a gift, I realized, as I began to recognize who my true friends were. People who truly have your best interests at heart don't care what car you drive or what materialistic items you possess.

## Money Makes Strange Bedfellows

The first day I decided to eat in the work cafeteria, I found myself sitting next to Brian, an engineer; Dani, a member of the camera crew; and Mad Mike, a technician with a temper.

They looked up in disbelief as my high heels pitter-pattered into the lunchroom.

"What's this? A bigtime anchor eating in the cafeteria with us peons?" said Brian, as the two others lifted their faces from their dinners, seemingly puzzled by my appearance as well. I ignored his sarcastic dig.

"You even have a designer bag to carry your food?" Dani asked, laughing.

"Oh, this old thing?" I said, slightly embarrassed at the small, inexpensive, multicolored cloth makeup case I had bought to use as a lunch bag. "The actual brown bags tend

## Chapter 8: Friends and Financial Foolishness

to leak," I coyly responded.

"Seriously, Romona, why aren't you out with the other network stars at a fancy restaurant?" Dani questioned, peeping up from her glasses to trade glances with the others.

"Oh, I get tired of eating out every night," I said, not revealing my true motivation. Had I told the truth, that I was trying to save money, I would have invited even more questions about my financial worth.

For twenty-four months, I resigned myself to eating in my office or I'd join my coworkers in the kitchen. It was a space large enough to seat ten comfortably, dressed in modern steel and light wood tables and chairs. I'd find a spot next to one of the regulars. I'd plop my frozen meal into the microwave. My mainstays were chicken and broccoli or lasagna and a healthy serving of raw carrots and broccoli. Sometimes I'd throw in my favorite lemon cookies. It was an easy ten-dollar meal, and it was also great weight management. Eating out nightly at restaurants with friends had been costing me about three hundred bucks a week.

I did splurge on the weekends, treating myself to nice meals, but come Monday, I was always back on track. I kept my eye on my end goal.

"I hope you guys don't mind if I join you," I shot back with an air of humility, looking around the room for their reaction.

"Nah, you're okay. We don't own nothing around here. We're just surprised you want to sit here with us," Dani continued. "You do have a nice office," she quipped.

"I get lonely in there. Besides, I need to see what y'all are doing in here," I said, smiling and making small talk.

It took them a few weeks, but we soon became fast friends, joking, talking sports and management, but mostly sharing about life and family.

My childhood stories are what seemed to quiet the room or bring outbursts of laughter. Initially, they didn't believe I actually had a pet pig that we slaughtered and ate for supper or that I chased down angry chickens and twisted their necks off. They couldn't picture their station's anchorwoman completing such gruesome tasks.

I think, like most, they just assumed I came from money. My position and power at work, my speech and etiquette, lent itself to someone of means.

It was during those dinner meetings that we realized our lives were somewhat intertwined.

Mad Mike never really shared tidbits about his personal life, but when he did talk, he spoke in an abbreviated way—never really finishing a thought. He literally was always angry at something—lazy, rich people; "cheapos" in management; or Cleveland's cursed sports teams, long before LeBron and the Cavaliers' 2016 championship win.

Pick a subject and he'd find something negative to say.

## Chapter 8: Friends and Financial Foolishness

We spent a lot of time envisioning our future after a hectic life in television news. Dani's mind was clouded with thoughts of having enough money to go back South, live mortgage-free, and raise a garden. Brian wanted the freedom to live a comfortable life—with no money worries: "Just let me go fishing and maybe own a small boat." Mad Mike mostly led the conversation back to his kids and their college fund. He and his wife were devoted to cutting back and socking away more for their kids' education and a nice retirement for themselves.

Our job titles and dreams were different, but our paths to achieve our goals were similar. Being a successful anchor, I was always hesitant to share what financial freedom looked like for me. I was fixated on saving up for a home, but I realized they wanted exactly what I wanted: to save enough money to live a worry-free retirement.

> **REFLECTION POINT**
>
> I want that for you too.
>
> - Take ownership of your money. Pay off your student loan and credit card debt, start to build a nest egg—all while having the bravery to ignore the lure of keeping pace with your friends.
> - Grow the bravery to stand in your truth and not conform to what society pressures you to be. The Bible speaks of this in Romans 12:2: "Do not conform to the pattern of the world" (NIV).
> - Feel comfortable saying to a friend, "I can't afford that right now."
> - Most importantly, stop lying to yourself about your finances.

## Friends and Money

Are you tired of watching your friends and colleagues build wealth that seems to have eluded you? Maybe you have money, but your careless spending habits and poor money choices have derailed your shot at financial freedom. Or are you just starting out your career and looking for guidance on how to set yourself up for success?

No matter your story or your income level, I take a dive into the deeper meaning behind why you might not be achieving financial success—and what you can do to turn things around and set yourself on a path to financial

*Chapter 8: Friends and Financial Foolishness*

freedom.

Trying to fit in with friends who have money you don't have can be daunting. Buying stuff, taking trips on credit, leasing cars you can barely pay for, renting apartments or homes you can't afford to furnish or keep up with . . . You can't spend all of your paycheck on these things and then blame someone else for your financial failure.

The Bible says:

> *Become wise by walking with the wise; hang out with fools and watch your life fall to pieces.*
>
> **—Proverbs 13:20 MSG**

I finally became money wise—both because of and in spite of the people around me.

Each month during those years, I'd put away at least 20 percent of my take-home pay. I was living a somewhat frugal life. Even though I'd sometimes splurge on something fun to enjoy, I mostly bought only necessities. I won't lie: It was tough to watch my friends buy brand-new cars, discuss their lavish vacations, and showcase their trendy bags and shoes. However, I had to keep my eyes on that two-year prize—saving for that 20 percent down payment. I did my own hair and gave myself my own pedicures. I could not pull off my favorite French manicure tips, so I still splurged on those every two weeks. I understand if some of you can't style your own hair. I grew up in a family with ten girls, and we made up an entire a beauty shop, styling each other's hair—the washing, the set, blow-dry, and curl.

In addition to my frugality and savings, I also immersed myself in soaking up knowledge about saving and investing. I subscribed to *Money* magazine, a monthly financial publication that featured everyday people from different socioeconomic backgrounds laying out their job titles, how much they made, and how they were saving and investing their money. Then they would have a financial expert give his or her advice on what the person should be doing with their earnings. There was always someone featured whose money journey meshed with mine, so I could learn from their successes or failures. Even during vacations, I would stuff that magazine in my purse to soak up information on the best credit cards, mortgages, insurance, and banking and investing advice. I was determined to learn what successful people were doing with their money.

I later became a huge fan of CNBC's *The Suze Orman Show*. Each weekend at 9 p.m, there I was, glued to my TV listening to the popular financial advisor dish advice on Roth IRAs, 401(k)s, the importance of having a trust and a will, credit card spending, delaying full retirement, and long-term care insurance. The information was dizzying, but I loved it. My girlfriend, however, was not a fan. She would complain we were going to be late to the club if I didn't start to get dressed and turn off that "loud-mouthed woman with the annoying voice," as she described her.

## Chapter 8: Friends and Financial Foolishness

"You're the only young person in the country watching that woman scream." But Suze spoke my language. It was as if she knew the financial path I was on and where I wanted to go. Each week there was something I learned to help steer me down the path toward prosperity.

Her pitch line—"People first, then money, then things"—ran parallel to how I lived my life, except I'd include God first. Those things worked for me. Find your own financial shows, books, or podcasts, and learn from them.

After six months, as I watched the money accumulate in my savings and investments, I began to enjoy its growth. It reminded me of my days of working in the garden with my mom planting vegetable seeds and watching them sprout and then harvest. Saving money produced the same kind of rush as gardening, knowing the sacrifices I made now would set me up not only to buy a house, but to weather the inevitable financial storms of life.

Finally armed with my down payment, I visited multiple banks. One lender told me I could afford double the house I was seeking to build. But Mom's money lessons were always in my ear about living below your means and making sure you save for troubled times.

That good sense, which she said God gives, told me to ignore the temptation of "more house" and envision my future the way I wanted it, not how others said I should live. It was a future that included not being house poor, but also spending money on experiences, helping family members and others, and giving to my favorite charities.

Learning not to be foolish with your money is not hard. It simply requires having a plan and changing your money habits. People who are good with money live within their means and are always looking to spend less than they need to spend.

Often it involves thinking differently from others around you. A lot of people justify overspending because they work hard and feel they deserve it. There's definitely nothing wrong with this, but you should find just one or two indulgences, then focus on bringing lunch from home or trimming your budget in other ways.

It also involves not worrying what other people think, no matter how much money you make.

## God's Wisdom, Not People's

The Bible has a consistent message about being wise with our money. We should save, but not hoard. We should spend, but with discernment and control. We should give back cheerfully, helping others, but with the understanding and the guidance of God.

"Porsche girl," to whom I referred at the beginning of this chapter, would spot me years later outside a mall getting out of my convertible, an S class Mercedes Coupe, and ask if we could hang out again. I noticed she was no longer driving her luxury car. I didn't need to know her story, but she was fixated on getting an update on mine.

## Chapter 8: Friends and Financial Foolishness

Replaying the experience in my mind, I can't believe I ever let her arrogance make me feel small. I didn't need to waste time on a shallow person who was too good to ride in my basic vehicle. So, I was cordial and just bid her good-bye. You can't be devastated when foolish people drop out of your life; they'll just hitch their wagon to the next big thing.

A few of those same people who had teased me about my cars and brown-bag dinners refused invitations to my housewarming party at my new home. Their faces said what their mouths could not—that they couldn't stand to see me win.

> *If you can't celebrate other people's success,*
> *you will limit your growth.*
> **—Unknown**

It's amazing how some people can't cheer on your success, but they're quick to discourage your dreams. I had to learn not to care what other people think. I have taken great advice and listened, but I ignored what was not meant for me. I seek the counsel of others and surround myself with people who are getting the money results I want for myself.

I learned to rely on God's wisdom and my own abilities and dreams—and to recognize Satan's lies. Satan wants you to be careless with your dollars, and that's when the corrupt swoop in to take advantage of you, enticing you with credit cards and get-rich-quick schemes.

Don't fall into the trap.

> *Dishonest money dwindles away, but whoever gathers money little by little makes it grow.*
> **—Proverbs 13:11** NIV

Start small. If you don't make enough to invest, a simple savings account is a good starting point. And concentrate on building up that emergency fund. I was stunned by the young people I interviewed for this book who had no savings accounts, or if they did, they used it whenever they wanted to buy something, which defeats the purpose.

It is financial foolishness not to save some of your hard-earned money for difficult times. It may be tough, but it begins with changing your mindset. Even if there is no money, push yourself to believe in the possibility. And if you change your mentality about saving, it then changes you. Soon you might find twenty-five, fifty, or a hundred dollars you can put away each month.

Some people called me lucky after I built my home. There was nothing "lucky" about being financially disciplined, sticking to a budget, sacrificing, and foregoing fun with friends—especially when you're young.

I've certainly made money mistakes, and you likely have, too, and likely we both will make financial mistakes again. But the key for me was to keep getting back up and getting back on track until I mentally fully adopted my new money mindset. It was only then that I started on this path of financial freedom.

*Chapter 8: Friends and Financial Foolishness*

Start now, wherever you are, and keep moving forward.

Don't get caught up on the age thing, either. It's never too late or too early to make a change. People may tell you how you're supposed to be doing at your particular age, but don't let that phase you. Stop being a prisoner of what society thinks about you. Set your goals, rely on godly wisdom, make a plan, and then stick to it.

Everyone wants to be seen as one of the cool kids. I get it. No one wants to be rejected because of their status in life. Rejection hurts us—pushing us to hurt ourselves financially. Once we start overspending, however, it can become a vicious cycle of trying to keep up.

## REFLECTION POINT

- You may have to love some friends from a distance or drop them completely.
- I had to learn through hurts and disappointments to surround myself with only positive, supportive friends—friends who listened, offered helpful advice, and pushed me in my journey to success.
- When you allow negative, gossipy friends to take up too much space in your head, you can fall into a trap of jealousy, doubting your abilities and simply being brought down to their level.
- I discovered some so-called friends were only happy when we were both struggling. When my finances began to rise, they started to project their limiting beliefs of upward mobility on me.

CHAPTER 9

# START EXPECTING THE UNEXPECTED

The Bible encourages saving, and even though you may hear more sermons about giving, God cares about saving too.

*The Message Bible* in Proverbs 6:6–11 uses the lesson of an ant:

*You lazy fool, look at an ant.*
   *Watch it closely; let it teach you a thing or two.*
*Nobody has to tell it what to do.*
   *All summer it stores up food;*
   *at harvest it stockpiles provisions.*
*So how long are you going to laze around doing*
   *nothing?*
   *How long before you get out of bed?*
*A nap here, a nap there, a day off here, a day off there,*
   *sit back, take it easy—do you know what comes*
   *next?*

*Just this: You can look forward to a dirt-poor life,
poverty your permanent houseguest!*

Ants intuitively look ahead, and in good seasons, they store up for more difficult days to come. The message the Bible seems to be saying to us is that what an ant does by instinct, people should do as a matter of common sense. This is a conversation I've had over and over with people who are in debt.

This is a lesson that is even more complicated for couples. Blending finances, and more importantly financial values, takes more time and communication than most people put into it.

I first met Carla in late 2019 at a Cleveland female empowerment conference. Her brows raised and her eyes widened when I started to talk about the third book I was writing, a book encouraging people to start saving more to create a path toward a more prosperous life for them and their children. After dishing out a few statistics on how Americans are not saving enough, I continued telling her why I was so passionate about the issue: People of color especially are not saving.

I could see in her troubled face that she was itching to tell me something. There was a short pause, and then, "I love it, Miss Robinson, but may I offer a suggestion?" she timidly asked.

"Sure," I responded. "I'm always open to ideas."

"Make sure you include a chapter on spouses who don't

## Chapter 9: Start Expecting the Unexpected

agree on spending and saving," she said, leaning to the side and inching a bit closer to me because of the ambience in the room. "My husband and I have been fighting about money," she confided. "Saving can be tough when one spouse feels like their hands are tied."

As lunch began, with no prodding from me, she started to tell me the story of her marriage. The relationship was on the rocks—not because of infidelity or a lack of love. Their problems existed over the almighty dollar and how to best spend it.

In this book, I wanted to share stories from other people's money paths to see how they were saving and spending their money. Carla and I agreed to meet and talk more after I started writing the book. Then the COVID-19 pandemic hit, and it shifted the tone of our conversation. As it did for many couples, the pandemic unveiled the money issues from which Carla and her husband had been hiding.

The stock market plummeted, businesses shut down, millions of workers were laid off or fired, and even worse, hundreds of thousands of people died of the virus. I watched cable news in horror and sympathy as people pleaded for help—begging for a financial lifeline.

"I've been laid off for two weeks, and if this work stoppage lasts more than a month, I don't know how I will feed my son. I have nothing," one woman said.

"My husband and I are both out of jobs because of this

virus. We don't have any emergency funds saved up," one couple said in New York.

"How are we expected to get buy for a few months with no pay?" asked a group of workers in Michigan.

The virus forced millions to seek unemployment benefits and to wait for a government stimulus check. The crisis revealed something deeper about our country. It's something we already knew.

As I said earlier, the average American family didn't even have four hundred dollars saved in an emergency fund, and that reality left many families ill-prepared for a crippling economic hit. With money already being the number-one stressor in America, most of our stress levels exploded during the pandemic.

## Carla's Story

That's what was going on when I finally talked with Carla a few months after the virus erupted in 2020, and she shared over the phone how the devastation was impacting her family.

"My husband has been laid off because of the pandemic. I'm still working, but it's not quite enough to cover our monthly expenses. We hardly have anything saved up. I'm embarrassed to say we only have about three hundred dollars in our savings account. We both have 401(k)s, but we don't want to touch those unless we absolutely need to."

## Chapter 9: Start Expecting the Unexpected

Their differing spending and savings habits were causing escalating conflict. "We fight over not saving anything, we fight over spending, we fight over how much debt we're carrying. I have about twenty thousand dollars in student loan debt; he has none. We fight over the boys' allowance. He gives his mom two hundred fifty dollars each month just because he wants to help her. I think he only should help her when she absolutely needs it, because we could save that money."

"Do you have enough left over each month to save at least something?" I asked.

"Sure, we do!" she said, the pitch of her voice rising. "We should not be operating in the red each month. We make good money. I'm a bank executive, and he's a manager at a car dealership. We live in a middle-class neighborhood. We're not living above our means. He does like to drive Beemers (BMWs). I have a Lexus. We have lots of money left over—each week about five hundred dollars in discretionary funds."

"That's two thousand dollars extra a month. Why don't you save some of that?" I asked curiously.

"That's exactly my point to him. I use about three hundred dollars each month on my hair and nails, and my fun money. I'm not sure where the remaining seventeen hundred goes. He's a shopaholic. He spends on the boys—too much if you ask me—and he brings home stuff that's still stacked in boxes in the basement and garage unopened. Plus, we are still paying off credit card debt from four years ago when we took the boys to Hawaii. I wanted to wait and save up for it, but he wanted to put the five-thousand-dollar trip on a credit card, saying we would pay it off with a thousand dollars a month. We still have a balance of about three thousand dollars on that card."

"What changed your payoff plans?" I asked.

"Bills. Sometimes you forget what it costs to own a home. I mean, until unexpected stuff hits you, like medical bills, plumbers, electricians, roofers, tree trimmers . . ."

"Do the two of you handle the finances together?"

"No, I keep the books by myself."

"Do you guys ever have budget meetings?" I inquired.

"Nah, it's more like budget arguments." An awkward silence followed. "Here's the real problem, Romona," Carla said, lowering her voice with a bit of emotion. "Kevin doesn't want anyone telling him how to spend his money."

Then she shared the roots of their differing money philosophies. "He was raised poor by a single mom in the inner city, and he wants to give our kids everything he didn't have as a child," she confided. "I've tried to put myself in his shoes and see how growing up in poverty left him feeling so depleted. I grew up in a middle-class home with my mom and dad, and I was taught to work for allowances and special perks."

## Chapter 9: Start Expecting the Unexpected

"I don't mean to pry, but I assume you have a bank joint account?"

"Yes, as a Christian woman, I don't believe in having a separate account from my husband. But lately, I've been asking God if maybe instead of pooling all our resources, we should each have separate accounts."

Then I overheard a faint voice on the other end of the phone: "Don't believe her, Romona. She's probably saying it's all my fault."

"Is that your husband?" I asked. "Can you ask if he'd talk with me?"

A few moments later, he agreed.

"I just wanna defend myself. She ain't telling the whole truth," he said.

"About what?" I asked.

He shared then about the pain of his childhood, filled with poverty and bullying—pain I'm familiar with. "I told myself that if I ever had a family, my kids would not go through what I did—being made fun of, having no money for school activities, dodging bullets and drug dealers. It was tough, but I made it. My wife, on the other hand, didn't have to worry about anything. Her mom and dad provided everything she needed. She took private swim lessons, fencing classes—I mean, come on, Miss Robinson, what black girl do you know who is a swordsman?" We all laughed.

"So, I do splurge on my sons, and she splurges on herself," he continued.

"No, I was not entitled, but yes," she said, "I do have a lot of nice purses."

As the conversation proceeded, we talked about how they had met and whether they had talked about money before they got married—no. Their first money conflicts were about the cost of their wedding. They talked about the debt with which they came into the marriage—her credit card and student loan debt—that had grown over the years, including the debt of his mother's car.

Parenting has only increased their conflict. "A few months ago, we argued about Michael Jordan tennis shoes our sons wanted. I said no, that they needed to earn them. They made a beeline to their dad, and he said yes! He bought the shoes—nearly five hundred bucks! That happens all the time."

"Our sons hear us arguing about money," Kevin added, "so I'm sure it's having an effect on them. The only thing we've ever agreed on is the money we've been socking away for the boys' college expenses."

Finally, we worked our way back to the present—they had little savings, were out of work, and had different spending habits. Carla said, "We're trying to adopt a new behavior toward money."

"How so?" I asked.

"I'm trying to convince him we can combine our

## Chapter 9: Start Expecting the Unexpected

attitudes about spending and come up with our own saving habits."

"Honesty is the best policy," Kevin chimed in. "I think that's where we've got to begin. Not hiding purchases and money from each other."

"We don't want this to ruin our marriage," Carla said. Her husband agreed.

Her husband added, "I've had time to sit, listen, and think over this conversation. All those 'things' I bought only brought me short-term happiness. I know we need a concrete plan to save for our future." Kevin's voice was resolute and eager. "I'm home now without a job, with a fancy car in the garage that I drove to a boring job I didn't even like. We have a crazy amount of debt, partly because I've been trying to make up for childhood deficiencies."

"Imagine the peace of mind you'll have once you have a nice cushion of cash, something to tide you over in an emergency," I added.

As we ended our conversation, Carla said, "This has been one of the calmest conversations we've had about finances in a long time." They both chuckled.

If you're struggling with managing your debt, you can get great advice at consumerfinance.gov.

If you plan to get married someday, do not skip the marriage counseling sessions with your pastor or visit with a marriage therapist. It's vital to talk to someone about all aspects of marriage and money. They will encourage you to talk about your finances, your sex life, your plan to have children—everything. If you don't get this counseling before marriage, you may be in for some shocking surprises.

Opposite styles often lead to friction, which is why money is consistently one of the top-two causes of marital conflict. Experts say being transparent about your finances is crucial before and during a marriage.

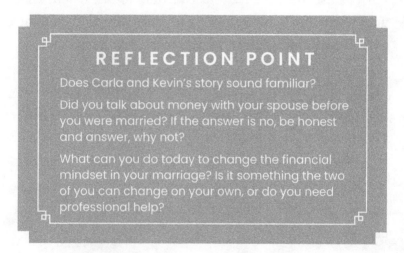

### REFLECTION POINT

Does Carla and Kevin's story sound familiar?

Did you talk about money with your spouse before you were married? If the answer is no, be honest and answer, why not?

What can you do today to change the financial mindset in your marriage? Is it something the two of you can change on your own, or do you need professional help?

CHAPTER 10

# SHOW ME THE MONEY

*Formal education will make you a living; self-education will make you a fortune.*
—**Jim Rohn**

One of the rewards of being a journalist is that you gain knowledge about a number of different subjects through years of reading and interviewing people.

In 2002 I traveled down a one-lane road lined with a burst of fall colors produced by mature trees. The tiny, quaint town housed a bakery, a diner, a florist, and souvenir shops. The idyllic scenery was pretty and peaceful, but the story I was about to hear was anything but. I was in small-town Ohio going to meet Debbie for a story I was doing on financial insecurity and seniors. Debbie was a seventy-three-year-old widow who described herself as someone who could twist a tail to explain her penniless predicament to friends. She was quick-witted and smart about avoiding probing questions. But in this interview, she wanted to tell the whole truth: why she was broke.

Debbie shifted back and forth in her chair, seemingly unable to find a comfortable position. Running her fingers through her natural graying, thin hair, then forcing them in her lap, she sighed heavily.

As we chatted, she told me she used to love designer makeup, perfectly coiffed hair, and manicured nails; she used to have an ostentatious wardrobe. But today there was no evidence of that previous life. She wore a plain, A-line-cut dress—pretty, yet simple. I complimented her on her Chanel shoes, but she quickly blurted out they were sixteen years old.

We were parked at a simple wooden, round table with four chairs with multicolored cushioned seats. The table was dressed with a white plastic table linen adorned with a vase stuffed with a few faux flowers. The adjacent kitchen was tidy, but small—the appliances dated. The hardwood floors looked original to her daughter's 1950's carriage-style home.

Her piercing blue eyes danced around the room—glancing back and forth at my cameraman and me. She shared she was searching for courage before sharing private details about her once–financially abundant life and how she had lost it all.

Signaling he was ready to start, my videographer raised his hand and indicated we should start. I began my questions.

## Chapter 10: Show Me the Money

Suddenly words spilled from her mouth about why she had been forced to move in with her daughter to make ends meet. She first wanted my word that I not identify her or the name of the town, where everyone knows everyone else. The story she told was one of intrigue, fear, and disbelief. Her new life consisted of divvying up her husband's monthly Social Security and pension checks to share in the rent and household expenses and help her adult daughter and granddaughter.

I asked her to tell me more about what had led to this point. Here is how she told her story:

"Surrounded by heart monitors, with oxygen hoses in his nose, and covered with pumps and cords, my husband revealed to me on his deathbed that we were broke," she said. He had suffered a massive heart attack, and the prognosis for recovery was not good.

"Crouched by his bedside, I recall vividly how he drew me in close in his weakened state to whisper that he was so sorry he had nothing to leave me. There was no money."

"Two emotions burned through my body over the next two days before he passed," she recalled. "At first, I was overwhelmed with grief. I was losing my husband of forty-four years. Then, I was consumed with anger. I was angry at him, as well as upset with myself for not knowing we had money problems and for never asking."

"I couldn't help it. I wanted to flood him with a barrage of questions: What? Are you sure? How can this be? How can we be broke? But I didn't ask any of those questions. I sat there perched next to him, holding and squeezing his hand. My brain went from feelings of deep sorrow to thoughts of the opulent lifestyle he had given me and our daughter. We had never wanted for anything.

"I felt guilty because my mind kept floating between caring for him in his final hours and memories of the successful life we had lived," she said.

They'd had a two-story, luxurious, suburban home, a manicured lawn, private schooling for their daughter, and lavish vacations. He'd worked most of his life in a corporate position that paid a low six-figure salary at the time of his death. Debbie had a degree in education, but she hadn't worked since their daughter was born.

As her husband lay dying, he told her about the bad investments he'd made and how he'd unsuccessfully tried to recoup his loses. He died without leaving her a will—nothing.

"At home, I ransacked his office," she remembered. "His file cabinet was cluttered with bills." In the weeks after he died, "I was racked with worry about living each day on the brink of survival. What was going to happen to me? Where would I go?"

Like Debbie, there are many women who are blindsided because they never had real money talks with their spouses. The weight of what was to come hit Debbie with brutal force.

## Chapter 10: Show Me the Money

Before she knew it, she was cleaning her own house for the first time in years and dreading checking the mail each day, finding late notices stamped in big, bold letters demanding immediate payment or face penalties. "I had never paid the bills before, and suddenly I was bombarded by the unfriendly world of creditors, prying friends, and overbearing relatives. When his job dropped off his personal belongings from the office, there was a mountain of letters from creditors. He apparently had used his office address to hide some of his other financial activities.

"It was humiliating. You can't even take a few days to process what has just happened to you because of the business demands, and the business was not simple. While I was at my most vulnerable, I needed to make choices that would have a lasting impact on my well-being. I was trying to make funeral arrangements, and I wasn't sure right away I was in charge of doing so. Friends offered to help, but I was bent on not letting anyone know just how bad things were. My pride would not allow me to ask for help. My daughter, forty-five at the time, was my rock, my sole confidante."

The result was a deep, complicated grief process. "He left me penniless and stranded, and yet I still loved him."

As time passed, she learned her husband had borrowed against the equity in their home to pay creditors, and his life insurance, in their daughter's name, was barely enough to bury him. Debbie spent countless hours searching for the paperwork that creditors demanded, all the while in shock, mourning his sudden death. "I was responsible for colossal household bills, and I was forced to cope with major life decisions when I was at my weakest."

Her face warmed, and a smile surfaced when she talked about their daughter. "She was a bright light in a dark and terrifying time. What she did for me financially and emotionally—" She used her index fingers to dry her eyes.

I was taken aback by her openness and willingness to share her story, which had happened only four years before. Despite it all, she had a sense of peace.

"I have calmness and love in my life now, but if you had met me right afterward, I was a crazed lunatic," she confessed, breaking a smile.

"Leaving the hospital, I got in my car and flung myself over the steering wheel in tears. When I pulled myself together and started the ignition, a hit song by Donna Summer came on the radio. You wanna guess which one?" she asked with a smirk.

"No," I said, shocked.

"Yesssss . . ." The word trailed as her bitter expression morphed into slight laughter. "She works hard for the money, honey . . . So hard for it, honey . . . so he betta treat her right."

"Then, without warning, there was this high-pitched howling, a pain that tore through my body. I belted out consecutive death-curdling screams as I shut off the radio."

## Chapter 10: Show Me the Money

"What is life really like now?" I asked.

"After the initial shock, having to sell our home for a loss, along with our cars and most of my prized jewelry, I feel free. Free of worry, free of the shame and embarrassment. I had the freedom to know I survived. When I think about all the sleepless nights, lying awake second-guessing my decision, or lack thereof, I feel the need to tell my story so other women don't make the same mistake. I don't have any of the same friends I had, but I guess they weren't friends anyway. If I was to be completely honest, I pushed them away. Without money I suddenly felt small, insignificant," she confessed.

Her husband's mistakes had had a lasting impact—and not just on her finances. "My situation threw me into a battle against anxiety, depression, and thoughts of suicide. For a long time, I was numb, but I thank God every day for my daughter and grandchild. I can't imagine having to take this journey alone."

"Any regrets?" I asked.

She paused, lifted her head in the air, briefly closed her eyes, measuring her words.

"I should have asked about our finances. I assumed we were on the road to live out our golden years financially secure. It never occurred to me to look at a single mortgage bill, retirement or bank statement, 401(k) statement—nothing. I mostly retrieved them from the mailbox, and not once did I ever have the inkling to peek inside. My husband handled our finances, and I just assumed we were fine. I did notice he seemed stressed a few years before he passed, but he always brushed it off as just having a bad day. Looking back, there are so many questions I should have asked, but that's not how I was raised."

She continued, "I mean, I'm not blaming my parents, but I was reared to believe that houses, fancy cars, and children equaled happiness. I was encouraged to marry a man who could provide those things for me, but neither Mom nor Dad ever said, 'Make sure you track your finances.' I assumed it was normal to let the man handle the money, and the woman focused on caring for the house and kids. That's how my parents lived, and theirs before them."

I had one final question. "What would you say to a married woman or man in her thirties, forties, fifties, or any age?"

She paused. Her eyes shifted to the side again and became moist with tears.

"Tell your spouse to show you the money you have. Don't rely on their word that your finances are okay. It's not that you don't trust them, but there are things you would need to know in an emergency. If they refuse, there is something wrong there. You should know if you have a life insurance policy and if you're the benefactor. Make sure you're okay if, God forbid, something unexpected happens."

*Chapter 10: Show Me the Money*

Though these can be tough conversations, she urges, women especially, to protect themselves: "Don't be scared or timid; ask questions. I learned through therapy, which my daughter paid for, that having conversations about death is a gift married couples give to each other."

> **REFLECTION POINT**
>
> - Ladies, please stop saying you aren't good with money and allowing someone else total control of your finances. This is a lesson for both men and women.
> - Even if one spouse keeps the books, they should be open to the other. Transparency is a must.
> - You should know if you have a life insurance policy and whether you are the beneficiary.
> - You should know how much your retirement nest egg is. Ask questions, and actually look at the financial statements and documents.
> - Unlearn the behaviors set upon women that they are not good with money.
> - I had to unlearn the values of being a quiet, good person, and learn to self-advocate, promote my own capabilities, and get guidance when things became difficult.

CHAPTER 11

# PROTECT WHAT YOU EARN

As far back as I can remember, even when I was five years old, Mom would drag us to church revivals at other sanctuaries.

There is nothing like a room-rattling revival with black folk getting' happy. The pastor was running around like a man possessed. He huffed and puffed, stomped, and kicked his legs in the air, sending the congregation into a shoutin' frenzy. The blaring sound of the organ whipped the people up into a celebratory dance—some with raised arms running up and down the aisles crying out to God. Others were spinning around in circles, arms outstretched and flapping like a bird about to take flight. This was unlike any church service I had ever visited. I was an impressionable child, and I soaked in everything I witnessed.

It started off normal enough. We arrived in the

church's gravel parking lot, and it looked like most rural churches—a modest chapel encased by part–grass, part–gravel and concrete slab leading to the entryway. We would usually have to assist old ladies who found it difficult to balance themselves as they clutched their Bibles and tiptoed around rocks and gravel to avoid scuffing their Sunday shoes.

Inside, though, there was something waiting I've never erased from my memory.

I'd spent my entire childhood watching church confessions about actual miracles, but I had never seen one take place right before my eyes. I prayed and prayed, asking God to save my mom from poverty, yet all her adult life, I watched work and worry rob her of any joy. *Where was her miracle?* I thought. I didn't understand why God's promises were not manifesting in Mom's life. Sure, she was blessed to have a job and to be able to care for her children, but why the constant struggle?

That day, the preacher asked parishioners who wanted a miracle to come forward. He wailed, "Come, come on, whatever ails you, God can fix it!" A hoard of people rushed to the altar, stretching out their hands, hoping God would hear their cries and bestow favor.

One woman, in particular, in a wheelchair, planted herself right at the foot of the pastor. He tucked his Bible under his armpit and placed his other hand on her forehead. He shouted out a few verses of Scripture, then told her to "get up, get up. You can walk now!" She rose

## Chapter 11: Protect What You Earn

and took a few steps, to the roar of the congregation. The next man said his body was riddled with cancer, and the pastor flung open his Bible, reading from the Good Book a few inches from the man, then announced, "You are healed!" He slapped the man on his forehead and shouted, "The cancer is gone! God has cured you!"

He then asked us to place money in the plate being passed down the pews for God's miracles.

The minister just waved his hand over the people's heads and peddled promises of prosperity and good health—but it seemed to come at a financial price. My sisters and I would giggle because he looked more like a man cursed by the devil than touched by the Holy Ghost.

On the drive home, I was astonished by all I had seen, and I asked Mom about the preacher's instant healing powers.

"Don't you believe any of that s&#!—that man is a crook," Mom said. Mom sure did curse a lot for a Christian woman when she was angry, but we were never allowed to.

"How do you know he's crooked, Momma?"

"I just know. I can see it all in him, and I just know. He claims he can talk directly to God so he can swindle people out of their money. Shame on him, taking advantage of poh people."

It was the first time I had witnessed ill-gotten gains. Mom would go on to explain to us that there are good churches and good pastors led by the Spirit of God and we should be careful in choosing when we were older.

Mom possessed the gift of discernment. She always prayed and waited on God before making big decisions. She avoided a lot of major money mishaps by being able to judge a person's true character.

She could see through the lie—and so can God.

> *The heart is deceitful above all things, and desperately wicked; Who can know it? I, the LORD, search the heart, I test the mind, even to give every man according to his ways, according to the fruit of his doings.*
> **—Jeremiah 17:9–10 NKJV**

You can't fool God. He sees your motives. You can't pretend to be loving and giving and have a deceitful heart. He knows the root of things in your heart when you give and help His flock. If you're doing it to gain trust, influence, or financial gain, He knows.

And if you trust God and open your eyes, you can spot people who try to impress you with big words and educated double-talk. My mom spent the whole car ride home that day making sure we'd never get tricked.

"You've got to be careful wit' yo money and make sho the preacher is truly anointed by God and not a sham. There are good pastors out there, but others will steal yo money."

That lesson also applied to people who were peddling

*Chapter 11: Protect What You Earn*

promises to fix whatever ailed us. Jehovah's Witnesses would knock on our door pushing their beliefs. Others would come by selling lotions and potions to instantly cure a cold. Mom would slam her door shut right in their faces and forbid us to open it. I used to think it was rude, but Mom was always exhausted and said she didn't have time for liars and cheaters.

> *Look at that man, bloated by self-importance—full of himself but soul-empty. But the person in right standing before God through loyal and steady believing is fully alive, really alive.*
>
> —**Habakkuk 2:4** MSG

## Cheated

Those lessons along my journey would stick with me.

Living life by the Bible also taught me that the bad deeds of others eventually catch up to them and they fail—like the lender who cheated me and hoards of others.

In 2003, I received a suspicious letter in the mail. It was an official-looking white business envelope. A thin green strip of paper ran across the front attached to it, which read in big bold black letters: *YOU COULD BE PART OF A CLASS-ACTION LAWSUIT.* My reporter radar was immediately heightened, since I had read countless stories about scams and frauds. I almost tossed it after a quick glance. Thinking back, I'm not sure why I didn't. I took the bait. The letter informed me I could become part of a nationwide class-action lawsuit. It stemmed from the home I had purchased more than a decade earlier. If I had received a home loan from the aforementioned bank, the letter said, I could fill out the paper work and send it back to participate in the lawsuit.

I was suspicious when it said I could receive thousands of dollars. I mean, who was trying to scam me, trying to get my personal information? I wondered. I called the number on the letter and learned it was legit. The banking institution that had once held my mortgage was found negligent for charging blacks higher interest rates and fees compared to white borrowers who had similar credit profiles. I would later read that it was because they felt blacks were more likely to default on their loans. I was livid. How could they do that to me because of the color of my skin, and not my credit score? I had perfect credit—the highest FICO score you could achieve—and I'd put 20 percent down, and yet that didn't matter.

Thinking back to how hard it had been to save for that down payment, I began to seethe. All the sacrifices of not eating out with my friends, missing out on fun trips, and brown-bagging it to stash away cash. Never being delinquent on my bills. Putting aside extra funds for maintenance, repairs, insurance, and furniture.

I filled out the paperwork and ultimately received a hefty check in the mail. The payback was satisfying, but I was still upset that blacks could be the targets of such

## Chapter 11: Protect What You Earn

unfairness.

> *Even on their beds they plot evil; they commit themselves to a sinful course and do not reject what is wrong.*
> 
> —**Psalm 36:4** NIV

Eventually I reported the story on our newscast after a nationwide settlement was reached. The lender was slapped with multimillion-dollar fines and millions more in settlements to black homeowners. I know there was also an apology, the exact words of which escape me, but there always seems to be an excuse to justify racial bias. I was upset that in my excitement to buy a home, I had allowed myself to be taken by ignoring one of Mom's cardinal rules: Watch your money; people will cheat you.

> *Better to have little, with godliness, than to be rich and dishonest.*
> 
> —**Proverbs 16:8** NLT

I had allowed myself to be conned by kind, yet dishonest words. I remember vividly the day it happened. I was about to do something I had dreamed of, prayed about, and saved for for years.

Driving to the bank, a huge smile on my face, I admired the fiery fall leaves, bursting with color. It would be my second home purchase, but this one was special. I'd get to work with an architect and decide its look, size, the floor plan, the lot size. Every interior finish would be hand-picked my me, from the flooring down to the doorknobs.

After saving and sacrificing for two years, I was ready to build my dream home. I was nervous about the size of the mortgage and the enormity of the moment, but I was mostly elated. My joy had me floating across the parking lot to the door of the bank, knowing I had done it. I had achieved my monetary goal.

As I walked in, I was greeted by a woman who introduced herself as the manager and said she had been expecting me. It's been more than a decade since that day, but I can still hear her voice—soothing, inviting, and trusting. Her pale skin against a red scarf framed her oval-shaped face and expressive, friendly eyes. We exchanged compliments while I followed her to her office.

As I waited for her to pull up the numbers and get the paperwork in order, my mind ventured off to the girl who had grown up with a dozen people crammed in a one-bathroom house. I was about to build a five-bedroom home, with no less than six or seven baths, I had told my builder.

As my architect designed my house, he questioned, "Good Lord, you're single. How many bathrooms do you need?" But that was my splurge. I didn't need more than even one bathroom, but I wanted them.

Years earlier, I'd pledged that if I ever bought a home, it would have enough bathrooms that when Mom and my siblings visited, no one had to wait for long periods of time. As a child, I remembered the wait was unbearable. You needed a strong bladder to survive the harsh reality

## Chapter 11: Protect What You Earn

of waiting in line until it was your turn. I'd prop myself against the wall outside the bathroom crying, fearing my bladder wouldn't hold. I squirmed, paced, and jumped up and down in place. My shoes stomped the hardwood floors, creating a noise that I hoped the bathroom occupant would hear, then take pity on me and let me in.

There was a hierarchy in my family as I grew up. My older siblings ranked first in line, hogging the bathroom, each saving entry for the next oldest. I was right in the middle—child number six—so if their time included a bath, well, I was out of luck. Occasionally, the pecking-order playbook would be thrown out, and a younger child, prone to accidents, got to cut in line.

Some mornings, I'd march in place beside the bathroom door until someone handed me tissue paper and yelled, "Go outside!" It didn't matter—rain, snow, or shine—I spent a lot of time outside becoming one with nature.

If you've never done your business outside on a farm, trust me, you want to go quickly. When I think back, I can see myself as young as four, squatting outside, legs and knees trembling while trying to balance my tiny body. There were no bushes in the backyard, so I always had an audience of chickens and hogs.

Even bathing at night was like waiting in line at the only women's lavatory in a busy airport. Some nights I took "birdbaths" in Mom's big, steel, three-gallon bucket if the kitchen sink was taken.

So, as a prospering adult, I was determined to have enough bathrooms in my new house to accommodate my family when they visited—no one would ever have to wait.

Seeking my loan, I first started with one of the banks I had a credit history with since arriving in Cleveland. But when the banker showed me the loan offer, I hesitated.

"Your loan quote is a bit higher than what was advertised," I questioned.

"Yes, those are for standard loans. You're getting a jumbo mortgage, so the rate is a bit higher," she explained.

I knew that to be true, but I didn't think it should be nearly 2 percent higher. There was that small, still voice in my head that said, *It doesn't sound right.*

> *"You shall not steal; you shall not deal falsely; you shall not lie to one another."*
> —**Leviticus 19:11** ESV

I shrugged it off. I was so excited about my home purchase, and I was certain an established bank like this wouldn't be deceitful. Not to mention, who would knowingly cheat a news reporter who could ruin them with just one story of suspected impropriety?

As a younger adult, I mostly took people at their word, believing what I saw on the surface. Not anymore! I always do my homework, especially when it comes to my money.

*Chapter 11: Protect What You Earn*

## Seeing the Truth

This incident with the mortgage company taught me that a liar's actions can mimic the truth. I had been conned.

The conmen themselves don't get off easy. Proverbs 13:11 admonishes, "Dishonest money dwindles away, but whoever gathers money little by little makes it grow" (NIV).

This same lender told me I could afford double the amount of house if I wanted to take out a larger loan. But I knew better than to carry that kind of debt.

The Bible spells it out: When you are in debt, you are beholden to the lender.

> *The rich rules over the poor, and the borrower becomes the lender's slave.*
> **—Proverbs 22:7** NASB

I would never live house-poor. I had been taught well about not overextending myself and always storing up for the storms of life. I could have bought a bigger house, a fancier car—maybe even two or three of them—but for me, being a prudent saver is tied to growing up without. I could not be seduced to overspend.

Besides, I had learned my lesson after being in debt. It can be dangerous. The lender has all the power over you.

After learning of my bank's deceit, I ended up refinancing and getting with a great lender that gave me a loan based on my financial history. There are many fair lenders out there—but you should still do your homework. It's reassuring to know today there are laws to guard against discrimination practices at federally insured banks (see www.fdic.gov).

God rewards those who are just and fair—those who listen to the voice of wisdom He puts in their hearts and who learn from their mistakes.

> *Whoever is generous to the poor lends to the Lord, and he will repay him for his deed.*
> **—Proverbs 19:17** ESV

When seeking a loan or committing to another financial agreement, ask lots of questions—of the lender, of your friends, of yourself. I discovered a wealth of information just by talking to people. Ask colleagues what they're paying for their loans and who their lenders are. A few of my white coworkers were generous in sharing information about the best lenders and the rates they received. That way, if you believe your financial life—your credit score, income, etc.—matches up with theirs, you can get a sense of whether you're being discriminated against in the loan offers you receive. Don't be afraid to ask "awkward" questions about finances, especially if you have a relationship with the person. Deceit thrives on silence.

Sometimes God may allow people to believe they are getting away with their misdeeds until His lesson is complete.

## Chapter 11: Protect What You Earn

*But if it's only money these leaders are after, they'll self-destruct in no time. Lust for money brings trouble and nothing but trouble. Going down that path, some lose their footing in the faith completely and live to regret it bitterly ever after.*

—**1 Timothy 6:9–10** MSG

Just as important as making sure you aren't being cheated is making sure you don't become a cheater yourself. Going down the path of lying and cheating to enrich yourself is not resigned to businesses leaders.

Over the years, I've heard a few people talk of enjoying a life of lies. They are caught up in cheating the system because they believe everyone else is doing it. People can get hooked on the "handout" that comes with government assistance. Some start falsifying their income or hiding cash to stay on that assistance. If they knew, as I do, that God is their Provider, they would not need to lie—because you can't fool God. If there is one reason for my lack of major money mistakes that could have devastated my finances, it's knowing from where my Help cometh. When you stop believing the Lord is your Provider and shift your eyes elsewhere—Satan wins. That is what he wants: godless people who will cheat, steal, and kill for money.

## REFLECTION POINT

I wanted this chapter to highlight the deceitful heart of people when it comes to business dealings—financial transactions we all make every day.

*The heart is deceitful above all things, and desperately wicked; who can know it? I, the Lord, search the heart, I test the mind, even to give every man according to his ways, according to the fruit of his doings.*
—**Jeremiah 17:9–10 NKJV**

If you trust God and open your eyes, you can spot the people who are trying to impress you with big words and educated double-talk. In addition, follow these proven sound principles:

- No matter your story or your income, you must protect what you earn.

- If you're tired of watching your friends and colleagues build wealth while it seems to have eluded you, chances are, they control their money; it does not control them.

- Maybe you earn plenty of money, but your careless spending habits and poor money choices have derailed your shot at financial freedom. Stop throwing away good money and look for ways to turn things around with professional guidance on how to set yourself up for success.

## CHAPTER 12

# CHASING MONEY INSTEAD OF LIVING

Years ago, my husband, Rodney, won two coveted club seats—near the fifty-yard line—to wach his beloved Washington Redskins play football. (I have since converted him into a rabid Cleveland Browns fan!) In one game he attended, the roar of the crowd was deafening. Competing against the Jacksonville Jaguars, the Redskins had the ball in their end zone. They were threatening to score and take the lead.

Beyond excited, Rodney was high-fiving strangers, when he reached over to slap the hand of his buddy, a coworker—only, Bill was still seated and busy tearing open a package of crackers he'd brought to the game. Everyone in his office at the Department of State in Washington, DC, had been clamoring to go to this game, but Rodney didn't think long about who he wanted to bring along with him. He chose Bill, one of the nicest guys in the office;

they both worked as IT contractors.

"Hey, man, what are you doing?" Rodney had to raise his voice over the crowd. "They're about to score!" Rodney looked down in disbelief at Bill and the crackers, then motioned for his buddy to stand up and join the other eighty thousand ravenous fans who packed the FedEx Field.

It was the third down with one yard to go, and the quarterback, Brunell, was behind center, ready to receive the ball.

"Come on, man, get up! We're gonna get something to eat in two minutes, as soon as this quarter ends," Rodney pleaded.

Bill awkwardly scrambled to his feet, shoving his crackers in his pants pocket, just as Brunell overthrew into the end zone, missing his receiver. The quarter ended.

"Aww, man," Rodney echoed with the crowd. "Let's go to the concession stand and get something to eat." He slapped Bill on the back.

"No thanks, I brought some crackers," Bill replied.

"I'm about to get a beer and a burger—don't you want one? Crackers are a pretty light dinner for a two-hundred-pound man. You didn't have to pay for the tickets, so let's just get a beer!"

"Nah, you know me, Rodney. I don't spend a dime." Bill stepped back, allowing Rodney to pass.

## Chapter 12: Chasing Money Instead of Living

Minutes later, Rodney returned with two beers and two plates of burgers and fries. "I gotcha dinner, man."

Looking grateful for the gesture, Bill quickly grabbed the meaty sandwich and tossed back down the beer. Bill made a six-figure salary, and yet it pained him to spend a dime. He wore run-down shoes, and his clothes were at least ten years old.

Bill was popular among his colleagues. His red hair, fair skin, light smattering of freckles, and boyish grin matched his pleasant demeanor. But opposite Bill's delightful demeanor was a man obsessed, fixated on storing up wealth.

At forty-seven years old, Bill was a single guy—he lived with a pet monkey named Charley. He worked long hours, stressed about downturns in the stock market, and never ate out or took vacations. He was cheerful in the office when his investments were up, but he was clearly tense when they were down. All hours of his day were consumed with making money.

One day Bill walked into the office, and his pale cheeks were damp with tears. Rodney assumed there had been a death in the family and expressed his concern. Bill confided he had just lost a lot of money in the stock market. His darkened, tense expression and blotchy, reddened face was a clear sign he was wound too tight about his finances.

Bill coveted and saved most of what he made. He never

splurged on anything or enjoyed the fruits of his labor. He never joined the group for lunch in the city, instead brown-bagging it at his desk. His vacation days were lost each year—because he refused to take any time off. He was the lone man out when it came time to support the company's charitable campaign. He never participated in the office's toy drive at Christmas.

Charley, his monkey, was the only known splurge in his life—ever.

Bill did have a girlfriend of twelve years, but he never married her. Rodney felt he feared that if things went south, he might lose half of his savings. "When are you going to make an honest woman out of her?" Rodney would ask.

"We both are too set in our ways," Bill would say, always cutting the subject short.

His conversations with coworkers were mostly about work, Charley—and, of course, his retirement plans.

"I'm going to leave this job early," he'd always say. "I want to take trips around the world. The first one will be to Italy, to a small village where my parents vacationed. They raved about it. Then I'll enjoy an adventure to Alaska to fish in Bristol Bay. I've read it's one of the best spots for fishing for salmon. I also want to see Ireland and Australia."

He had big plans.

Then one day Rodney arrived at work to find Bill's desk

*Chapter 12: Chasing Money Instead of Living*

empty. Bill was always the first one to arrive at the office and the last one to leave. The aroma of the percolating pot of coffee was always a sign Bill was already hard at work.

His coworkers assumed he had finally taken a day off or called in sick. But later, a hush fell over the office as they learned Bill had died suddenly—of a diabetic seizure.

The man who had been consumed with making sure he would never outlive his savings was gone in his forties. He would not live long enough to enjoy his retirement savings or achieve any of the things on his bucket list.

## Enjoy Life Today

The Bible advises storing away money for both known and unknown needs in the future. However, chasing the almighty dollar is not looked upon kindly in Scripture.

Jesus told the story of a foolish rich man in Luke 12:16–19 (ESV):

> *"The land of a rich man produced plentifully, and he thought to himself, 'What shall I do, for I have nowhere to store my crops?' And he said, 'I will do this: I will tear down my barns and build larger ones, and there I will store all my grain and my goods. And I will say to my soul, "Soul, you have ample goods laid up for many years; relax, eat, drink, be merry."'"*

You've heard the expression: "Money is the root of all evil." This seems to suggest that greed is the cause of a certain problem in someone's life or the cause of society's ills. That verse is often interpreted differently, but the Bible clearly says, "The love of money is the root of all evil" (1 Timothy 6:10 KJV).

> *Those who love money will never have enough. How meaningless to think that wealth brings true happiness!*
>
> **—Ecclesiastes 5:10 NLT**

When money is your god, you will always crave more of it. You will never be happy; you'll always be chasing more and more of it.

I guess we're all guilty of chasing money at some point in our lives.

As a young journalist, I'd work overtime, double-time, weekends, and holidays, thirsty for more and more money. However, that was because I made so little of it at the time. In 1983, I earned just under $15,000 at my first television job.

When you start to earn more, you realize that your family, health, and mental well-being are more important than working so hard for the almighty dollar. You relish your time off to have fun and relax. The high cost of stress is not worth the extra money to be made. Your spiritual and mental psyche are worth more than the extra cash.

When I was struggling financially, every time I'd hear the phrase, "Money can't buy you happiness," I'd always

## Chapter 12: Chasing Money Instead of Living

think, *Yeah, but I'd sure like to give it a try.*

From the time we graduate from high school until the time we retire, we are in pursuit of money. It's how we survive in this world. Getting rich was never part of my American dream, but it was central to the dreams of a few people around me. There was a relentless chase to become rich.

In their blind pursuit of wealth, these people became distant and moody, ignoring the people they loved, never enjoying life, just focusing on acquiring more and more of the almighty dollar.

As you are slaving away in the name of money, at some point, you have to ask yourself: *Am I happy?* Despite how powerful money is, it can't change the way you feel about yourself. You can't buy self-esteem. You can't purchase self-worth. No amount of money will erase a painful past or heal an emotional wound. Only you can do that—with God's help.

How many stories have we read about mega lottery winners who win millions of dollars but are broke in five years? God talks about this in the Bible.

> *"Whoever can be trusted with very little can also be trusted with much, and whoever is dishonest with very little will also be dishonest with much. So if you have not been trustworthy in handling worldly wealth, who will trust you with true riches?"*
>
> **—Luke 16:10–11** NIV

An acquaintance I knew who drank a lot came into a

huge inheritance. You'd think her newfound riches would have moved her to seek help, but instead she drank even more.

More money simply makes you more of what you already are. If you're kind, you become more generous. If you're a jerk, you become a bigger jerk. I've been witness to it.

I watched as wealth made some of my associates feel powerful. They want to be admired, but they become depressed when they were used for their money and dumped when the well ran dry.

God's Word promises peace and prosperity to those who keep their mind set upon Him; not to those who keep their minds only on their money.

Psalm 1:2–3 (TLB) says this:

> *But they delight in the doing everything God wants them to, and day and night are always meditating on his laws and thinking about ways to follow him more closely. They are like trees along a riverbank bearing luscious fruit each season without fail. Their leaves shall never wither, and all they do shall prosper.*

Deuteronomy 8 talks about God giving us the ability to produce wealth (verse 18), but the passage warns us not to put our hope in our wealth.

I have never been fixated on becoming wealthy, but I have always stashed away "fun money." There are some things about me that are undeniable—one is that I love

## Chapter 12: Chasing Money Instead of Living

flying first class (being upgraded to the first-class cabin is my "happy place" on trips over three hours), and I frequently stay at five-star hotels. While I don't crave the latest or greatest vehicle, the newest electronics or handbag is something I would occasionally splurge on.

I am nearly six feet tall, and my husband is six-foot-six, so flying coach is extremely uncomfortable for us. Because of that, I know the travel destinations remaining on our bucket list will be expensive. I still have South Africa, Jerusalem, Dubai, and New Zealand on my list. However, I know I can take those trips because I've done the financial work. I have gone without many other frivolous desires in my past to be able to afford these dream vacations.

Despite all of this, and although society puts a heavy emphasis on money and success, anything that truly matters is free—our breath is free; creativity is free; family, friends, and life itself is free. So is the freedom to put God before money.

Remember Abel in the Bible. He was a generous shepherd, who offered the fattest of his sheep to God.

> *But Cain, a miserly farmer, brought some of the fruits of the soil as an offering to the Lord.*
> —**Genesis 4:3–4** NIV

God accepted Abel's offering and rejected Cain's—an indication that Abel was more righteous than Cain.

God's blessings are meant for us to enjoy and share,

not stash away for later.

> *"Lay not up for yourselves treasures upon earth, where moth and rust doth corrupt, and where thieves break through and steal. But lay up for yourselves treasures in heaven, where neither moth nor rust doth corrupt, and where thieves do not break through nor steal."*
>
> **—Matthew 6:19–20** KJV

First Timothy 6:9 (MSG) says this:

> *We entered the world penniless and will leave it penniless.*

God doesn't want us to be penniless and broke while we are here on the earth. He wants us to enjoy life with the fruits of our labor. If we're not careful, though, money blinds us to what's really important—living life with joy and peace and helping others along the way.

CHAPTER 13

# THE POWER TO SAY NO

If you were to ask me what is one of the most important lessons I've learned on my money journey to a prosperous and financially independent life, without hesitation I would say it's being comfortable saying the word *NO*.

I have said no to careless spending, no to living above my means, no to jobs that were not a good fit for me, no to repeated loans to people who used me, no to business opportunities that would overload my personal time, and no to career opportunities that paid well but that I new were disasters waiting to happen. Does any of this ring true for you?

I shared earlier that after I graduated from college in Jefferson City, Missouri, I couldn't find a job in my field. I sent out dozens of résumés to television stations in and out of town seeking employment. No one would hire me. I was living with my sister and brother-in-law, and I knew I would have to get a job soon to earn my keep. So, I applied for a job at what was then the Sears department store, and I was offered manager position, making a $25,000 annual salary. That was a lot of money in 1982. But I put off accepting the position, because I did not want to give up on my dream of becoming a journalist. I had to believe God had not brought me that far to abandon me.

And it's a good thing I waited—because soon afterward, I would be offered a part-time job at a local radio station. But the salary was only $4,500 dollars a year. I wrestled with my decision. Sears was offering four times more money. I could live very well on that in small town Jefferson City. If I took the radio job, I'd have to continue camping out at my sister's place. At least, however, I would be working in my field as a radio and news personality, even if the salary stunk. And, I reasoned, I could continue to send out résumés—only now I would have a radio air-check to showcase my talent. I said no to Sears.

Four months later, I was offered a lucrative, high-profile job.

I still remember the day I met him. His piercing, bluish-green eyes and power suit exuded an air of confidence as he walked into the radio station to be interviewed by one of my colleagues. As soon as we were introduced by my news director, he locked his eyes on mine and lingered, making me a bit uncomfortable. He was a well-known politician. I can't recall what was said, but there was some small talk, and then he asked if he could speak to me in private after his interview. "Sure," I replied.

## Chapter 13: The Power to Say No

What he had to say surprised me. "I have been looking for a new chief of staff for my campaign, and you might be perfect for it," the politician said. I found the offer highly unusual because he had just met me.

"Really?" I responded, puzzled.

"You're educated, you're an articulate journalist, and you seem as if you'd be a good fit for my campaign. I can pay you over thirty grand, and I know you're not making nearly that here. Let's schedule a sit-down at my office next week."

*Wow*, I thought to myself. *I could instantly increase my salary—five times what I'm making now.* I had never been offered a job opportunity so quickly, especially without an interview. I felt like shouting *yes* to his offer immediately. I could move out of my sister's house, finally afford to live on my own, and start to build a career in politics—but then there was that tiny voice in my head that was cautious. An even bigger voice reminded me I had craved becoming a TV news anchor since I was six years old. The lure of more money can be so tempting. However, I could see in the politician's eyes that he liked more than just my professionalism and articulation skills.

> *"If they listen and obey him, then they will be blessed with prosperity, throughout their lives."*
>
> —**Job 36:11** TLB

It's tough to obey God's warnings when the seduction of money and success can lure you down a path of lust for the things in this world. Saying no to a much higher salary may seem insane, yet God knows we will come face-to-face with the temptation of money, which is why He speaks so often about it in His Word.

A week later as the politician urged me to take a seat and talk things over, that uncomfortable feeling crept through my body—deep within my soul this time.

He praised my looks, along with my radio show, then started in with questions that were way too personal, including what part of town I lived in and whether I would be able to work late nights and travel out of town with him on a whim.

I sat through the interview, but I knew I was a child of God, and as it says in the *Message Bible*:

> *Less is more and more is less. One righteous will outclass fifty wicked, for the wicked are moral weaklings but the righteous are God-strong. God keeps track of the decent folk; what they do won't soon be forgotten. In hard times, they'll hold their heads high; when the shelves are bare, they'll be full.*
>
> **—Psalm 37:16–19** MSG

I might have been struggling financially on my meager radio salary, but my decision to decline that offer from the politician would pay off. A few weeks later, I was hired at KRCG-TV as a reporter in Jefferson City, Missouri. My

## Chapter 13: The Power to Say No

initial salary was $14,500. It was half of the money I'd turned down, but as I explained in my memoir, God had granted me my dream job.

Had I not followed the godly wisdom within and said no to his offer, I might have missed the TV opportunity and gotten tied up in an uncomfortable situation, all due to the lure of more money.

Proverbs 1:8 (MSG) begins with a warning about temptation:

> *Pay close attention, friend, to what your*
> *father tells you;*
> *never forget what you learned at your*
> *mother's knee.*
> *Wear their counsel like a winning crown,*
> *like rings on your fingers.*
> *Dear friend, if bad companions tempt you,*
> *don't go along with them.*

Think about times when you've agreed to do something, whether in your professional or personal life, and you later resented yourself for saying yes. How you wished you could go back and say no.

I encountered this numerous times during my career in the newsroom. When asked if they'd work weekends, work early morning hours, or take on an extra shift—the people who weren't afraid to say no did so—especially if they felt the boss was repeatedly asking them. Those who wanted to say no but were afraid to do so would then misplace their anger and become upset with their colleagues who had declined the offers for overtime. When they did that, they were giving the impression their answer would never be no.

I had to learn early in my career and personal life that it is okay to say no when it applies to your money, your time, and your mental well-being.

I've talked to several people who, like me, regret not having the power to say no to things that were stunting their future financial plans. Jessica's fear of saying no could have ruined her financially.

By all accounts, Jessica had it going on. Well educated, she was one of the youngest women to work her way up to a vice president position at local bank. She was socking away money and living the good life.

My talk with her was riveting.

I met her in Cleveland nearly twenty-five years ago, when she was an intern at one of the TV stations I worked for.

She kept in touch over the years as some of the younger journalists do, seeking mentorship and advice. She switched careers to go into marketing and then banking in Chicago—which was where she finally found her niche.

At the age of forty-five, she had purchased a home in the Windy City. She had invested for her retirement. She was living life on the fast track to having it all. Except for what she always wanted—a family.

## Chapter 13: The Power to Say No

That is why she said yes, even when she knew the answer probably should have been no. She met a successful entrepreneur whom she described as both smart and funny. "Romona, he loves me, and he is so easy on the eyes," she raved. "But there's something that's bothering me."

Her pause over the phone gave me cause for concern.

"What's bothering you?" I asked.

"He wanted me to help him with his new venture to open a gym, and I did. Even though we had only been dating a year, he convinced me to use the equity from my house to get a one-hundred-thousand-dollar loan to help him with repairs, equipment, and opening the business. I know I should have said no, but I was afraid the relationship would sour if I did. I'm ashamed to admit, we got the business open, but it was a flop. Now the money's gone, and I'm no longer sure about the relationship. The love I had felt so strongly has grown into resentment, fear, and regret. Looking back, when he said he'd pay back the loan, I should have sought legal advice and gotten it in writing to protect myself. I honestly don't think I'll ever see any of that money."

Jessica took a huge financial hit to her quest to become financially independent by fifty-five, but thanks to her years of saving, she'll bounce back. She'll just have to work a little longer past her planned retirement age.

David was a fifty-one-year-old divorcée who bought

his kids everything they wanted—in many ways, to make up for the divorce. Now he wishes he had said no more often. He provided instant gratification for the kids, but he has left himself without a safety net and the savings he needs in order to build their futures.

"The word *no* just didn't seem to provide the comfort they needed," he said. "Their mother and I have been divorced five years now, and they still seem to have trouble adjusting."

David knew he needed to draw the line. He felt he needed to buy his children's affection to make them "like him more." He knew that needed to stop.

Our inability to say no often stems from the fact that we want to reassure others and make them feel comfortable. This, however, isn't always a good idea. Yes, if there is a family emergency, of course you can help, but just giving money away in order to "people-please," or putting someone else's needs before yours to make them like you, does not add any value to that person's life or ro yours. Trust me, I know it's not easy when you have the money and a friend or family member has a need but beware when they start coming to the well too many times.

Mom taught me to never lend money to anyone. I went against her teachings a few times, and I was always upset when the loan was never repaid. She was adamant: "If you can't afford to lose it, don't lend it. If you want to help someone and give them money, then just give it to them. But don't expect it to be returned."

*Chapter 13: The Power to Say No*

Women especially tend to overextend themselves trying to achieve a work-life balance. How many obligations can you juggle—and likely drop—before you say, "Enough, I can't do any more?"

A friend of mine literally became bedridden for two weeks because she was so overworked and overbooked. She held a full-time job; she was a wife and a mother of four kids; she participated in nearly all the church groups and school activities; and she would never say no to many more obligations. She was pulled in so many directions that she eventually fell both mentally and physically ill from total exhaustion. She was off work for weeks—and she had to take unpaid leave, causing financial loss.

Saying no changes people's expectations of who you are. If you become the go-to person for everything, they will always continue to ask. If you're recognized as the cash cow, they will avoid asking others completely and only come to you. And they will always expect the answer to be yes.

*No* is a powerful word—it's no wonder so many people are uncomfortable saying it! It may sting at first, but "no" is not always a negative thing.

*No* can force people to branch out on their own and explore opportunities to create a better life for themselves. It can spur them to get out of that hole they've dug for themselves.

Saying no to the things that are not good for you frees

you up to say yes to things that are infinitely better for you.

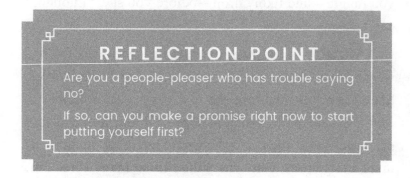

**REFLECTION POINT**

Are you a people-pleaser who has trouble saying no?

If so, can you make a promise right now to start putting yourself first?

PART 3
# THE PAYOFF?

# CHAPTER 14

# TO WHOM MUCH IS GIVEN

*We make a living by what we get,
but we make a life by what we give.*
**—Winston Churchill**

Once we reset our money mindset and begin to build our wealth, our work isn't done. In fact, I believe it's only beginning. If you are the person waiting on God's promises, this chapter outlines why *He* may be waiting on *you*. I believe God holds us responsible for what we've been blessed with—and not just our money. He wants us to use our talents, our knowledge, and our time, not just to enrich ourselves, but also to benefit others.

This is not a story about how you should be giving all your money to charity and the Church so that God will bless you. It's about using what God has given you and being a good steward of it—whether you have a lot or a little (but especially more than enough). As a journalist covering manmade disasters, I have so often watched the poor outgive the rich in times of crisis. Maybe it's because they know the pain of going without.

Of all my accomplishments in search of prosperity and purpose in my life, the one that gives me the most gratitude has been the ability to help others.

As soon as I started to earn success, I knew I had to continue to live by the verse in the Bible that says, "To whom much is given, from him much will be required" (Luke 12:48 NKJV).

After all, I was raised among people who had very little but who gave a lot. Their generosity lives within me, along with what the Bible says about wealth.

I know you might be thinking, *Well, what if I am not a religious person?* That's okay. You don't have to be religious—all you need is an open and giving heart. You need a heart that says, "I'm blessed and doing well, and I want to help others in a way that I see fit."

For me, though, God is important in my financial success. For so many years I thought God was only building my television career. Unbeknownst to me, He was building my brand, my following, for when He would be ready to use me for His purpose.

God already knows everything about you, what you will do with the wealth He bestows on you. He knows your potential and abilities. He especially knows what's in your heart.

## Chapter 14: To Whom Much Is Given

He brings your provision, and He can dry it up. He knows that if He can't trust you with a little, there is no way you could manage a lot more.

COVID-19 provides a great example. During the pandemic, God forced us to see the problems of the world—the sickness, the hunger, the health disparities, the massive loss of jobs and financial resources. He forced us to stay at home and "talk" to each other. The racial unrest we saw on our televisions made us want to be more kind, to listen and learn about the struggles of people who don't feel safe in their daily lives. People who have never felt valued and who continue to fight for equality that's seemingly always out of reach. I believe God is asking us to stop, listen, and act.

> *"Divide your portion to seven, or even to eight, for you do not know what misfortune may occur on the earth."*
> —**Ecclesiastes 11:2** NASB

The Bible doesn't tell us it's wrong to be rich. But if you are trying to create wealth, there are certain expectations it sets forth.

> *Command those who are rich in this present world not to be arrogant nor to put their hope in wealth, which is so uncertain, but to put their hope in God, who richly provides us with everything for our enjoyment.*
> —**1 Timothy 6:17** NIV

During the pandemic, it was gratifying for me to witness people with tremendous wealth come to the aid of those less fortunate and those with little sharing what they had as we all struggled to get through the crisis together.

I believe God was asking those of us who were able, to be a blessing to others, and many people responded.

Thirty years ago I truly began living a purposeful life. It was the start of my first TV anchor job in Cleveland, but I also spent countless hours volunteering to work on behalf of others. There were days I would come into work exhausted, having already volunteered at two charity events before my ten-hour shift even got started. I recall one week when I had logged about six or seven events already, and I expressed to my colleague how exhausted I was, hoping to garner a few words of encouragement to continue my work. Instead, he said something I've never forgotten: "Better you than me, Romona. How come black people feel this responsibility to give back and help other blacks when they become successful? White people don't have that pressure."

Floored by his shallow remarks, I chose to just keep on walking down the hall. It was clear he knew nothing about the history of my race—or his own.

My focus had to remain on my purpose and the work I wanted to do, especially for women and children. I wanted to continually be pouring into others what God was pouring into me.

## Chapter 14: To Whom Much Is Given

In 1990, I started a TV segment called "Romona's Kids." Its purpose was to give a voice to youngsters who didn't have one. I wanted kids who were growing up like I did to know they had a shot at success, and I loved highlighting the volunteer work being done in their schools and communities. I also loved going to the more prominent schools and showcasing the work they were doing. I showcased kids who knew the power of giving and helping to change the world through civic responsibility. My segment would become an institution in Cleveland. It is one of my proudest accomplishments as through encouragement and simple kindness, I have been able to reach children some said couldn't be reached. These kids deserved a chance to change.

I remember listening to an interview with a woman who was being asked for a donation to help a mother and her seven kids, and she replied, "Didn't nobody tell her to have all those babies if she can't afford to take care of them!" As Christians, is that the way God wants us to respond to the hardships of our fellow human beings? To the hardships of children who, through no fault of their own, simply need a helping hand?

Some of the kids I've talked to over the years did not get any hard and fast expectations or advice from their parents about achieving success, so they fell behind. Does that mean we abandon them when we ourselves have something to offer? We can give of our time, mentorship skills, encouragement, guidance, and yes, finances, to support programs that feed them and meet their needs. Money gives you the power to change lives, shift mindsets, and lighten the burden of shame that others without it may be experiencing.

Volunteerism has been a huge part of my journey in serving God. But it is the faces of the people I have served that have left a lasting impact on my life.

Four-year-old Brandon was a rambunctious preschooler who was frantically pulling boxes off a store shelf as I assisted him. I was participating in a holiday Shoes for Kids giveaway for children in need.

I patiently placed Brandon's discarded shoes in the proper boxes as he mindlessly searched for the special pair he wanted. He spoke few words; he just huffed and puffed, looking for a pair of Power Rangers shoes in his size. His eyes lit up like a Christmas tree, and he let out a yell when he found them and clutched them close to his heart. Right there in the aisle, I helped him slip the prized possessions onto his feet. "Thank you, thank you!" he exclaimed as he looked up at me. "I never had shoes like this before!"

"You are welcome," I said. "A lot of goodhearted people made these shoes possible for you." I could tell my words weren't registering by the puzzled look on his face. He was just grateful for the gift.

His joy drove my mind back to a time when I was his age.

## Chapter 14: To Whom Much Is Given

As a child, I never experienced the joy of a birthday party or a new gift during the holidays—never. That might be hard for you to believe, but it's true. Raising eleven kids as a single parent for most of her life, my mom couldn't afford to throw parties or buy gifts. Those were considered wants, not necessities.

Of course, that didn't stop me from dreaming.

Tucked away in my bed at six years old, I'd fall asleep dreaming about what it would be like if I were a little girl who got presents on Christmas morning. In my fantasy, this girl was a princess—a child of means and privilege. I'd envision her running down a grand curved staircase at midnight, like the one I'd seen in movies, eager to sneak over to the gorgeously decorated tree and open at least one of her many gifts. In my fairy tale, her mom would awaken and join her, allowing her to open "just one." The multicolored lights strung around the tree shined brightly, and different colors danced off the little girl's cheerful face. The princess in my dream knew Santa had come and delivered her gifts because she hadn't been naughty, but nice.

I'd imagine her opening the one gift to find the prettiest Barbie I'd ever seen. The doll had a pale face, the friendliest smile, and gorgeous brown hair, just like mine. They didn't make dolls that looked like me back then, but that was okay, she was a Barbie. I just wanted what every other girl at my school seemed to have.

However, that was just a fantasy. My siblings and I

were taught there was no Santa—no jolly, bearded fat man was going to come down the chimney and leave us gifts. Mom squashed any idea we'd have of ever receiving a gift at Christmas. It was hard to hear, but she reminded us each year that if she couldn't buy presents for all of us, she wouldn't buy them for any. And while she was resolute, I know it pained her.

In my daydreams, I could play make-believe, glorifying the good times that were coming, fantasizing about all the possibilities. I could wipe out the negative thoughts about how I'd never have what other kids enjoyed. I pretended better days existed and that they were coming, even though I knew they were not—at least not for a long, long time.

My imagination didn't include hand-me-down clothes or a shortage of food. In my world of fantasy, I could have a fast-food burger and fries—something I'd never savored as a child, only living vicariously through the mouthwatering stories from my peers of what it tasted like.

Some days my dreams felt like betrayals to my mom. She worked so hard to give us all she could. I appreciated Mom's hustle, the shelter and nurturing she provided for us, but that didn't prevent me from dreaming of a better life.

I used to cry out to the Lord and ask Him why I couldn't have presents like other kids, since I was a good girl too. Why my mom couldn't have something new and pretty, too. I used to tell Him it wasn't fair that Momma

## Chapter 14: To Whom Much Is Given

worked all day, her hands tired to the bone, and yet we still struggled. At the time, however, I couldn't see any way we'd ever have a different financial reality.

*****

So, there I was, vicariously reliving my past through the eyes of Brandon, a child who would get something bright and shiny, something new, that was just his own.

He had no way of knowing the joy I felt in my heart to witness the generosity of others who gave because they could and they knew God expects us to help.

Even though I had never had a new toy as a child, I could now feel the joy of putting new shoes on the feet of a child in need.

As I hugged him good-bye, Brandon would have no idea the joy that burned within my soul to witness his happiness, the tears I held back so as not to frighten him.

I've achieved tremendous success, but I care more about the children I've impacted and the lives I've touched. My life is about the legacy I want to leave. It's about using every tool in my toolbox to help repair broken dreams of women and anyone trying to fight through financial chaos and get ahead.

When it's my time to join my Lord and Savior and He asks how I used my God-given talents, whom I inspired, empower, and served, I want to have a good answer to give to Him. He won't care how many designer bags I owned, what type of Benz I drove, or how big my house is.

I take heart in hoping He'll say, "Job well done."

> **REFLECTION POINT**
>
> *The wise man does not lay up his own treasures. The more he gives to others, the more he has for his own.*
> —Lao Tzu
>
> Money is great, and it can open up many doors in your life, but it's not the end-all-be-all. True happiness—true wealth—comes from serving God.
>
> - You can be so blinded by the desire to make money that you forget what is truly important.
> - Abundant life is not about what we have. It's not about what we get. It's not about what we claim. Ultimately, abundant life is about what we receive as a gift from the Lord and living knowing we are stewards of the blessings of God.

# CHAPTER 15
# FINANCIAL FREEDOM

It took me a while to truly get it, but if I was ever going to reach financial freedom, I had to commit to becoming a good steward of God's blessings.

I've talked about old patterns of how we think about money and replacing the lies with the truth. But how do we achieve true financial independence? Drawing on my experiences, my faults, my challenges, and the wisdom both Mom and God gave me, I was able to make good money decisions.

I started with common sense. So many people say they know nothing about investing or the stock market. My "book sense" and talent got me far in my career, but it is my common sense I have relied on when it came to saving, investing, and spending my money. You've heard the old saying way too many times: If it sounds too good to be true, it probably is. Yet people still fall for scams, especially those with the lure of more money or get-rich-quick schemes.

I've always known the importance of saving, but I'd learn its true value after I left my anchor job in December 2018. While I'd been planning for some time and was confident in my financial future, others assumed I was on the brink of disaster.

"Romona Robinson is leaving Channel 19 News!" the newspaper headline read. "She is preparing to start a new season after 30 years in Cleveland television."

When I left that television anchor job, speculation immediately caught fire that I had been fired—even though the article rightly said I'd had a two-year plan to leave.

I was bombarded with questions of how soon I would sell my house—from people I knew and people I didn't. My husband was asked if he and I would be selling our luxury vehicles.

Curious home buyers stuffed letters in our mailbox asking if we were considering selling. Realtors bombarded us with flyers inquiring if they could represent us.

I would say I was shocked by the probing questions, but I was not. I was not even hurt by the curiosity.

Statistics show most people who experience an unexpected job loss or any other serious life hardship fall into financial crisis. They usually don't have enough of an emergency fund to get them through the storm. If they lose their job, they usually don't have enough resources to tide

## Chapter 15: Financial Freedom

them over until they can find a new job sufficient to cover the bills. Many end up selling their homes, downsizing their cars, or pawning precious possessions.

If you read *Your Voice Is Your Power*, you know that for most of my career, I had been planning for the day when I would leave television. And by now, you know I was raised to save for a rainy day by not falling victim to endless, mindless, extravagant spending.

Shortly after I left my job, I received a sweet private note from a young man on Instagram. He reached out to say he had just suffered a job loss right before I had left my own job. He thanked me for all my community service in Cleveland and wished me luck. He also wanted to offer me free rides. As an Uber driver, he was offering me free transportation.

"If you need a ride anywhere, I'm your man, Miss Robinson," the message said. *"I'll pick you up, take you anywhere free of charge. We cannot have our beloved television Queen of Cleveland suffering in any way."*

On the one hand, I thought, How precious! He cares about my well-being, or He's being a good businessman, offering up his services to a well-known celebrity. Or was there a deeper meaning to his remarks? Did he truly believe that after more than thirty years of steady employment, I had somehow been thrown into financial chaos and was in need of free transportation services?

An acquaintance of mine said she was not surprised at all by the financial inquiries and concerns. "Romona, most people, especially women, are not prepared for a huge financial setback, like the loss of a job. And if you're a black woman like we are, I'm not shocked at all that they believe you're about to suffer substantial hardship."

Women usually don't make as much as men for the same work, so to save a nice nest egg, we have to be especially prudent.

Saving is tougher for those in the workforce than ever before. Every generation seems to face more money pressures when it comes to their personal finances. Today, 401(k)s have replaced disappearing pensions. Health care, once paid for by your company, now requires you to foot a lot more of the bill. In the past, people had confidence that Social Security and Medicare would be around when they needed it—today, maybe not.

Over the last few decades, more of the saving responsibility has fallen on the worker. You have to create your own safety net.

It can take decades of consistent saving to build a healthy nest egg. Only you can decide how much or how little you're willing and able to sock away. I was shocked to read a bankrate.com survey that stated only 39 percent of Americans could afford an unexpected $1,000 expense if they lost their job.

I've heard people suggest that you should look at saving like a diet—you should spend less and save more, as in eat less, lose more.

## Chapter 15: Financial Freedom

I happen to think that's the worst piece of advice possible.

We've all done it. We start a diet. We're excited when we start to lose weight. We're mentally pumped that we can fit back in our tight jeans, but as soon as we see or smell our favorite fatty food, the cravings are back, and we fall off the wagon. We gradually fall back into old habits, and the weight piles back on.

The same applies to saving habits. You may be doing great for a few months, but then you see something you want and think, *Okay, just this one time I'll splurge and dip into my savings.* Before you know it, you want something else, and you've gradually depleted your account.

To save money for the long term, you must mentally adopt the same attitude that sustained weight loss requires. It's a mental commitment to be willing to change your money mindset to reach financial freedom.

Start with a simple first step: *Pay yourself first.* I immediately took advantage of automatic deposits at work, bimonthly. It was my way to funnel money directly into a money market account before I could see it or was tempted to spend it. I parked it there until I was ready to invest.

If you save just fifty dollars each month, you could have three thousand saved in five years. Plus, you'll earn at least some interest on that money. You already know this simple stuff. That's why I don't spend time in this book talking about *how* to invest your money; I know it will rub some people the wrong way, and that's okay. I hope to get under your skin a bit and push you to take a long, hard look at your finances, but I also hope to fill your heart with passion to change your financial ways and get on the road to financial success! I want you to have a cheerful heart when it comes to saving. I hope you know by now, this book is all about life, money, and how to handle God's financial favors on your road to financial independence.

I have talked to so many women and others who are afraid to invest. They will say, "I don't want to lose all my money in the stock market," so they keep their money in a savings account, CD, or money market account, earning meager interest all their lives. And that's okay if that money is enough to sustain you in your senior years to live a life of independence the way you see fit.

But in doing that, you may risk outliving your savings and being thrust into poverty as an older American, and that is a frightening thought.

I remember first sitting with my financial advisor at the age of thirty-two to draw up a plan for my money, and he asked, "How do you see your life as a retiree?"

"I want to quit working at fifty-five, have a huge house on the lake in North Carolina, watch the boats go by, and never have to worry about money," I replied. Only the latter is true right now in my life.

## Chapter 15: Financial Freedom

"Here's what we need to do and how much you need to save," he said. I balked at saving so much; after all, I was young and successful, and I wanted to spend my money and travel. But today, as a retiree, I'm so thrilled I listened to that man.

Ask yourself if financial freedom is truly what you seek. Are you willing to make some sacrifices and seriously engage in the practical steps that are needed?

The use of automated savings accounts was huge for me. If couldn't see it and I couldn't touch it, I didn't spend it.

I was recently listening to an interview with a musician who said something that resonated with me: "The reason not everyone is built for success is because not everyone is built for the struggle." The same applies to working toward financial freedom. If you want something bad enough, whatever sacrifice, whatever pain you have to go through, you do it, and you'll get there. But some of us are afraid of the pain that lies ahead. We're uncomfortable of going without, not quite believing we'll come out on the other end better, achieving our goals.

I started by setting a goal, and then I made an action plan and determined how best to achieve it. And when the moment came that I needed my savings, I was ready.

> **REFLECTION POINT**
>
> What would financial freedom look like for you? A mortgage-free home? Making $50,000, $100,000, or $300,000 a year? The freedom to travel without money being a factor? The ability to take annual cruises and see the world without it straining your budget? Paying cash for a new car without blinking? The ability to help others with simple generosity, not expecting anything in return? Volunteering or giving to your favorite charity?

## CHAPTER 16
# THE INHERITANCE

Part of financial independence means looking ahead to future generations and knowing there is a purpose to our wealth that will outlast us. My mom, who earned a meager salary and lived a pressure-cooker life trying to keep a lid on mounting bills and the demands of motherhood, had more money in her savings account when she died than nearly 58 percent of the people who live in this country. Her story is an example of how generational wealth is possible, no matter your income.

Mom summoned me back to her bedroom to talk privately. It was 2014, four years before she passed. I knew it was going to be serious if we needed to meet in the privacy of her room. That day I learned what she had accomplished financially by believing in God's promises.

"Look here, Romona. Look at this insurance paper," she said, wide-eyed, as she thrust a five-by-eight-inch certificate-shaped piece of paper close to my face. "This is my life insurance policy, and this is what I have saved up for you to bury me."

"Mom, I don't want to talk about you dying," I snapped, frowning and rubbing the back of my neck as I do when I'm uncomfortable.

"You listen—we need to talk about this. I ain't gonna live forever."

"No, Mom, can we do this later?" I suggested, sitting on the edge of her bed.

"Nah, it can't wait. I've put all these thangs in yo name. You just listen, you hear?" she said. "We need to talk about this now. I'm nearly eighty, and you need to know where thangs are." She sternly looked me straight in my face.

"Okay," I reluctantly agreed.

"Now, here's what I got saved up." She handed me another sheet of paper, and my eyes widened. "Yo name is also on my savings account."

"Wow, Mom, you saved all this?"

"Yes, I did." A big smile came over her face. She was pleased she had realized her dream and had a stash of cash saved up to leave for her kids.

"You've known since you was little I wanted to leave my kids something," she said, tilting her head to the side with pride.

I stared at her, thinking, *What a woman!* She had fought

## Chapter 16: The Inheritance

to survive most of her life, but all she could think about was leaving something for us—and she did.

"I want you to withdraw this money and divide it with yo sisters and brother when I'm gone. You split it equal."

"No, Momma, I don't need anything. I don't want anything," I responded with authority.

"You listen to me, I want you to have somethin'. You take yo share, you hear me?" She was adamant.

I sighed. "Yeah, Mom," I said reluctantly.

A sadness came over me, as I realized Mom was preparing for the end. I somehow used to feel that if you talked about dying, you would jinx things and the person might actually die soon after. But the biggest smile covered Mom's face the whole time she talked about the inheritance, small by some standards, she had amassed. For a woman who had labored so hard for so little, for so many years, it was a big moment.

I can still hear the tone of resolve in her voice as she made clear how I was to carry out her final wishes. She was thinking about the health and wealth of her kids.

Proverbs 13:22 (ESV) acknowledges the value of such a legacy: "A good man leaves an inheritance to his children's children."

In those beautiful moments, I could see Mom's deep love for her children.

The woman who earned meager money on the assembly

line had made it a point to educate herself on financial literacy through the memories of her dad's teachings, the rich man she had worked for, and most importantly, her own godly wisdom. She then passed down that knowledge to us. The inheritance was important because she was leaving generational wealth—ensuring we had something to tide us over in hard times, a gift most black parents could never afford to give.

The latest figures from the U.S. Census Bureau show the median net worth for an African American family is now $9,000, compared with $132,000 for a white family. Latino families did not fare much better at $12,000.

An inheritance is not just about money. My siblings and I also inherited Mom's financial wisdom, integrity, self-discipline, and responsibility, which were vital to ensure we would manage the blessing long after she was gone.

Mom saved money, acquired burial insurance, and had her house in order so she dind't burden her children when her time came. She earned somewhere south of $5,000 annually, yet she had far more money put away in a savings account than most people who live in this country do. In 2018, 58 percent of Americans had less than $1,000 in a savings account, according to a GOBankingRates survey.

The methodical, mental, and consistent way she saved left a permanent mark on me, and I knew if she could do it, anyone could. For a long time, I didn't have much empathy for people who seemingly did not try to save and instead offered excuses—because I had watched

## Chapter 16: The Inheritance

Mom sacrifice and put money into savings. Over time, though, God opened my eyes and my heart, allowing me to see those struggling through the lens of their good and bad choices and not simply my own judgment. Yes, there are those who can save but don't—both rich and poor—but reliving visions of when Mom barely had enough, I realized it can be degrading to tell an impoverished person to "just save."

We were blessed to live in a rural community. Raising thirty farm animals to supplement food in the inner city is not possible. Growing a large garden requires time and space.

It's hard for the poor to win when the cards are stacked against them. People who read my first book raved about how I picked myself up by my bootstraps and worked hard to achieve success, but I never owned boots—Mom couldn't afford them. I remember the cold, wet, snowy earth seeping through my worn penny loafers that were no match for whatever frigid mix Mother Nature served up.

No, I didn't have boots, but what I did have was the mindset to believe I deserved more.

No matter how hard Mom tried, things always happened to set her back. She always seemed to stay afloat because she never lived above her means. Yes, it was a somewhat frugal life, but we got the things money can't buy— love, security, and a parent who was there for us. Knowing what I know now, I'd choose a nurturing parent every time over a rich but absent parent. Mom was never drowning in debt.

She didn't go out to bars; she stayed home with her kids. Our entertainment was the radio—when an occasional hit played that we loved, we'd all jump up and dance. I never ate out at a restaurant as a child, and shopping was reserved for needs only.

## Lasting Lessons

In 2018, after God took Mom home, I reminisced about a woman who gave up the best years of her life to ensure her kids had a fighting chance at success. I carried out her financial and funereal wishes. I found myself caught up in strong memories of her hard-earned godly wisdom about money.

Poverty was all she ever witnessed or lived, yet she was fiercely strong, and she taught me more basic money lessons than any degree, job, or setback in my life ever could. Like a warm spring day with the perfect breeze, her face possessed a radiant glow during our monthly mentoring sessions when she filled out those bank deposit slips. "Now, listen, Romona, you always keep track of yo money. So, you always write down how much you deposited, what day and time it is, and the check number, you hear?" (Thank goodness, computers and apps make keeping track of our checking accounts simpler these days!)

Months later, at home feeling proud that Mom had fulfilled her dream, I found myself thinking back to Mr.

## Chapter 16: The Inheritance

McKay, the rich man from whom she'd learned a few life and money lessons. I wondered if his four sons had received the inheritance he'd promised. They would have been between sixty and seventy years old themselves.

Mom's gift to us was probably minuscule compared to Mr. McKay's bequeathed wealth, but she believed in family supporting family, and we all learned that lesson.

I come from a close-knit family. When you make it, you reach back and help others. The generational philanthropy began with my eldest sister, Mary Jane, who married young and started a family. She would buy clothing and other items for me while I was in college. After my sister Beulah graduated college, she'd send money back to help Mom with our younger siblings. When Debra came out of college, she got married and started a family—she'd also send home money to Mom. Brenetta graduated college two years before me as a home economics major, and she made special-occasion outfits for me to wear during my junior and senior years. Evonne married right out of high school and left for Hawaii. She would help me while I struggled financially through college; she'd have given me the shirt off her back if I'd asked for it. When I got my first job after graduation, I, too, helped the family out financially, and the legacy of giving continued. Helping family members who were helping themselves was Mom's spiritual money mantra. It shaped my thoughts about earning, saving, and sharing my blessings with others.

## It's Not Just about You

Here's what I know after several decades of saving: Those God-fed teachings propelled me to use my prosperous life to spread hope, faith, and purpose in not just the lives of my family members, but in the lives of other people, as well. That's the beauty of attaining financial freedom: It allows you the opportunity to lighten the burdens of another. You realize it's not just about you. God wants to shift your thinking.

The COVID-19 pandemic has been a reset for us. As we were stuck in our homes, families were allowed time to look at their budgets, prioritize their finances, and rethink their spending habits.

Financial freedom means different things to different people. Not everyone wants to be a millionaire. What life would you like to design for yourself? Do you want the freedom and flexibility to do what you want when you retire? The choices you make today directly impact your ability to attain those goals.

I've talked to several people who make six figures who don't have a good financial outlook because they've given in to a higher lifestyle than they can afford, spending almost all they make. And this affects their stress levels and their ability to reach their goals.

When you hear people say, "Money doesn't bring happiness," what they're really saying is that it won't cure

## Chapter 16: The Inheritance

what ails you—anxiety, depression, loneliness, you've got to tackle those things. But trust me, when you live a life of financial freedom, you will increase your happiness and reduce your stress. You won't be racked with worry when the market crashes or when there are massive job losses—and rest assured, there will be more financial shocks in the future. Having a cushion to weather the storms allows you to sleep at night, and should you do lose your job, it gives you the freedom to take stock of the situation and decide what to do next instead of panicking and jumping at the first job opportunity that comes along.

When you have a safety net in place, you almost always have more options. It affords you the freedom to decide what job you want to pursue. That money gives you peace of mind to take your time and figure out your next steps, instead of being under tremendous pressure to react quickly to everything that happens.

I now walk in "mature money faith"—I made that up myself. This occurs when you realize "you grown" and you don't have to prove something to someone else or to society. Some people scoffed at me when I wore my niece's five-dollar paparazzi jewelry at the anchor desk. I laughed and shrugged off the comments. When you get to a point that how you spend your money is your own business and you aren't concerned with what others think, that's "mature money faith."

Financial freedom is more than just having money. It's the freedom to be who you really are and do what you really want to do in life, following your passion, making choices that aren't determined by your bank account, and living life on your terms. More importantly, it gives you the freedom to help others through giving generously whenever and wherever you see fit.

> **REFLECTION POINT**
>
> I found that the more I provided service to others, the more my blessings grew. Will you make a commitment to build generational wealth for your family right now? Starting today?

## CHAPTER 17
# MY TRUE WORTH

By now you understand how I developed my character, bravery, and the power to prosper. It was always within me—powered by the wisdom God gives all of us.

I am also very much my mother's daughter—minus the cussing. My tone is not as bold as hers, and I do have more of a filter, but her courage runs through my veins.

It's why I'm not afraid to go up against injustice.

I learned that God gives you all the tools you need to win a fair fight.

Like the one waged against me when I was seeking a raise at Channel 3—the story I shared at the beginning of this book.

The ultimatum had been issued. There were six months remaining on my contract. I'd been told the station would move on if I didn't accept their latest offer. Even though persistent rumors that I might be replaced moved swiftly through the newsroom, I remained resolute.

As I waited for God to reveal Himself in the situation, I won't lie, there were days when my anxiety trended toward panic. I have had several bouts of stress throughout my career, but nothing like the heap of doubt that crawled through my brain day in and day out during that time. Where was the tough girl I told you about earlier? The one who said she could sell herself better than her attorney? The one who was raised to believe black women were strong, that we don't give up without a fight? The one who said anxiety was for other people—that she didn't need therapy and pills for what ailed her? The woman who believed that if you put your trust in God, all things are possible?

Painful memories of being out of work in the past invaded my confidence, eroding the gutsy and faithful person I had become.

I would awake at 4 a.m. some mornings and question God. The question I couldn't silence in my mind: "Would he really replace me?"

Station brass even paraded a few female candidates through the halls when they brought them in for interviews, making sure the right person spotted them, ensuring word would get back to me. These not-so-subtle maneuvers were put in place to remind you to stay within the box management was comfortable with you staying in.

And like the busybodies they were, the gossipers couldn't wait to tattle.

## Chapter 17: My True Worth

They cornered me in the hall. "I saw a gorgeous woman heading toward the elevator this morning," one colleague said, champing at the bit for a reaction. "You didn't hear this from me, but I was told she'd interviewing for an anchor job." His eyes bulged as he looked straight at me, waiting for a reaction. There was none. I smiled at him and said something to the effect of "Good for her," as I exited the elevator.

It was all designed to rattle my cage—mentally and emotionally—and it did.

A few days later, I was summoned by the GM—after the caravan of my potential replacements, each more beautiful than the next, I was told.

I knew this was management's test to see how I was holding up. With my unsigned contract tucked underneath my arm, I prayed for strength and courage as I prepared for what would likely be another verbal showdown—and the end of my career at Channel 3.

I usually wore two personas when I negotiated my contracts. I could be the darling in the room if I was treated fairly, but if there was any hint of patronizing the pretty little anchor, then Mom would emerge. I would relive all Mom's lessons about being enough, earning your keep, competing with everyone else by becoming more knowledgeable, and probably the most important—never let nobody make a fool of you!

On this day, the GM motioned for me to sit on his more

comfortable, tufted black leather sofa, while he took a seat in the adjacent matching chair. I glanced over to the wall of windows overlooking Lake Erie. The waves crashing against the rocks seemed to match the chilly and rocky atmosphere that had ensued during our last contract talks.

"Have you thought about our offer?" he asked.

"Yes, I've given it a lot of thought, and I can't sign this," I said as I handed the contract to him.

He refused to reach for it. Instead, a frown covered his face as he rubbed his chin in frustration. The tone in his voice was a little deeper and more intimidating.

"I am going to offer you what I think is an excellent deal for you. I want to give you one more chance to sign it," he stated, leaning forwarded sternly.

My body didn't seem to work after his words were delivered. Fear had frozen every natural movement.

Then suddenly, I remembered my roots. When you live in poverty, you become good at hiding the brokenness inside. You put on your smile, cover your wounds, mask the hurt, and go out, letting the world see only your confident exterior. So I forced something that mimicked what I should be doing. I cracked a smile without showing my teeth—my mouth literally would not open. I tried softening my brows and resting my arm on the couch.

I was going up against one of the most powerful forces in television, but then I remembered the power of God. All I could think to do was cast my eyes to Him. "Dear

## Chapter 17: My True Worth

God, help me. This deal is unfair, and he knows it."

"This is it, Romona," he said. "I suggest you talk to someone about this. It's a good deal. I'll give you a few more days to decide."

My heart felt like it was drifting in a land of nothingness—open, barren, lost somewhere in the desert.

Again, I reiterated my desire to remain at the station and help with its continued growth, but at a salary in line with what male anchors were paid.

He reiterated that I'd been misinformed, that no one made what I was asking. "Have a good weekend," he finally said with a blank expression. "We'll talk again next week. I expect your final decision then."

I rose from my chair to exit, my frustration and fear building. I had to remember I wore the armor of God and that "no weapon formed against me shall prosper."

Still, fear can grab you by the heart and you can start to second-guess your decision. Voices in your head can encourage you to cave and accept a bad offer.

> *The gullible believe anything they're told; the prudent sift and weigh every word.*
> —**Proverbs 14:15** MSG

Suddenly, I felt the weight of my entire career in my hands.

Word had gotten to me that a few other local stations were interested in me if I decided not to stay. They could not tamper with the negotiations and talk to me, though. That would have been in breach of my contract. However, I had spent my career moving to and from four different stations, accepting offers that I knew were below what I should be getting paid. I had just accepted it because I was so thankful to have a job in the business. However, a transformation was taking place inside me, one that said I needed to address the unfairness—first, because a raise meant securing my financial future, and second, because I knew I would start to become angry, feel underappreciated, and seek out other jobs I might not enjoy as much. I would end up repeating the same pattern, just at a new location.

Feeling defeated, I stopped in the ladie's room on my way back to the newsroom to gather myself. I was thankful I was alone. As I stood in front of the wall of mirrors hunched over the sink, I was too scared to look at myself. I didn't want to see the fear that I knew had ravaged my face. As much as I tried to hold it in, I couldn't. My surroundings in the lavatory became a blur, and so did the sound of foot traffic in the hallway. The pressure of the moment became too heavy to bear. I recall doing something that was completely out of character for me. I became a fire-breathing dragon—letting loose several curse words. For a minute, I had become a clone of my mom, using language I didn't know I possessed.

This was different from anger-filled words I had used before. Profanity-laced verbal projectiles were being fired from my mouth with ease. I took some deep breaths,

## Chapter 17: My True Worth

trying to hold back the feelings raging inside me, but I couldn't. I raised my head, and a few tears traced down my cheek—and just like that, the floodgates opened.

The last three months had worn on me. The stress I had been carrying was a like powder keg that finally blew. I had chosen to go it alone without legal representation, and the negotiations were kicking my butt—and my midsection. The too-tight red suit I wore was evidence of that. My face was more rounded, my body a bit plumper. I had gained weight eating my go-to comfort food at bedtime—vanilla ice cream with crunched-up barbecue potatoes chips. I needed the snack to calm the stress before trying to sleep. My brain scrolled back through all the times I had been told what I couldn't do because of where I lived.

Crying had always been a healthy release for me, so that tear-filled moment and profanity fit served as the fuel I needed to gather myself and stand strong.

I could not and would not let them see me crack under pressure. I had to believe that with God it wasn't over yet.

## God's Angel

"Romona, Romona!" a woman excitedly called as I was about to open the door at a Cleveland suburban mall.

I turned to address her as she huffed and puffed, out of breath after sprinting across the parking lot to catch up to me.

"Do you remember me? Do you remember my

name?" she asked, raising her hands to her face in joyful anticipation that I might recognize her. "I met you at my high school. You were there to speak to the kids and was looking for the principal. I'm the custodian you met that day. You were so nice to me."

It was Saturday morning, a day after the meeting with my boss when he had announced they would move on without me.

I had spent the night trying to control the chaos running rampant in my mind, fearing I might be fired.

I had resigned in my thoughts that God's inaction was, in fact, His answer and that I should consider signing the deal. Maybe the person, though credible, who had shared with me my research and Q-score in the market had been mistaken like my GM had suggested.

"I voted for you," the woman continued with supportive pride on her face.

"You voted for me?" I questioned, confused.

"Yeah, everybody voted for you."

"For what? What do you mean?" I persisted.

"They showed us a video and asked if we recognized you and the other anchor people on the screen, and if we did, what we thought of each person. We all loved you— black, white, young, old. Everybody loved them some Romona," she exclaimed.

In all my years in television, I had never before met

## Chapter 17: My True Worth

a viewer who had participated in a television focus group. It's a huge part of the television market research method, which brings viewers together in a room to provide feedback regarding TV talent. There are usually thirty to sixty people polled, with different attitudes, feelings, beliefs, experiences. The station is looking for what viewers like and don't like in a newscast and its personalities. Based on that research, the leading talent in the market is determined.

Most anchors have a strong niche audience—a certain group that loves them. It's rare to appeal to every demographic: black, white, brown, male, and female in the coveted twenty-five- to fifty-four-year-old age range. Almost never would they all give the same person high marks.

My lips curled into a smile as I basked in her kind words.

I wasn't sure why I felt like I was somehow cheating, but I kept seeking more answers.

"What are some of the questions you guys were asked?" I pressed.

"They asked us why we watched Channel 3. Some people mentioned the weather and talked about that man, the reporter they don't like, but everyone said you were the biggest reason they watched the station."

"C'mon, everyone?" I continued to pry.

"Yeah, we all raised our hands and told them the same

thing."

"Do you remember the people leading the group?"

"I don't know names, but they introduced themselves as the 'bosses' at the station. One guy said he was with the corporation."

My first thought was that I had stumbled on a gold mine of pertinent information that confirmed what I had been told. God had provided confirmation in the form of an unlikely source.

"You are really popular, Romona," she said in parting.

She had no idea why I gave her one of the biggest hugs I'd ever shared.

She was the angel God sent to reignite my fire to fight with everything I had to be paid fairly and equitably.

I believe that when you start to lose your faith and then find it again, God rewards you with favor. I'd spent my entire career dealing with things no young woman should have to endure, as I chronicled in by previous two books: sexual harassment, racism, and sexism. I was doing a whole lot more work for less money and being underpaid and undervalued.

Moments of weakness and fear, which had smothered my thoughts with doom and gloom, were swept away, and my faith was reinvigorated.

> *You are my refuge and my shield, and your promises are my only source of hope.*
>
> —**Psalm 119:114** TLB

## Chapter 17: My True Worth

On Monday, as I walked into work, I wore God's armor of strength. I carried a bold, confident, and cheerful exterior as I strode in. It was a stride filled with confidence in God's promise to never leave me nor forsake me. And the pep in my step did not go unnoticed.

My assistant news director commented, "You seem awful chipper. Nice weekend?"

"As a matter of fact, yes, I *did* have a nice weekend." My coy smile screamed, *I know something you don't.*

A few hours later, when the news open-rolled announcing CHANNEL 3 NEWS AT 6 STARTS NOW, I came out of the gate with a noticeable dose of exuberant energy, confidence, and poise. I purposefully kicked it up a notch. It was a strong performance—I was engaging, my ideas were thought-provoking, I was asking probing questions of reporters. I was clicking on all cylinders.

During the newscast, the assistant news director came into the studio while we were on a commercial break and asked that I go up and see my GM right after the show. "Okay," I responded, a little nervous about the timing. Unless you've slandered someone or made a huge error in reporting facts, any minor problem with the GM is usually handled through email or can wait until the next day.

It was about 6:45 p.m. He stood as I entered his office—waving his hand for me to sit in one of two chairs in front of his desk. His posture was relaxed as he reclined back in his seat. My heart rate was off the charts as I pulled back a chair to sit. *This must be it*, I thought. *He wants to know my answer. If I don't accept the offer, I'm out, and they're moving on.*

"I just got off the phone with corporate. I want you to know this was tough to get. But I fought for you because you are an integral part of our team, and we want you here. You'll get your raise. You deserve it."

My eyes seem to stretch to the size of golf balls. I couldn't believe what I had just heard. I didn't know whether to scream or to cry—my initial thought was that neither was appropriate or professional.

I had put some padding on the number I had asked for so I'd have some wiggle room to negotiate. Yet, they were agreeing to the full amount.

"Congratulations," he said. "I'm thrilled you are going to remain part of the team."

"Wow," was all I could muster, followed up with, "Thank you—thank you for fighting for me." I was still trying to swallow my excitement and keep my emotions at bay inside my body while I was in his presence.

My mind raced back to all I had endured, all the stress, the sleepless nights, the bouts of depression and fear.

"I'll have this drawn up in the morning, and we can wrap it up," I recall him saying with joy in his eyes. He looked relieved or tired of fussing with me—maybe both.

*Chapter 17: My True Worth*

# The Payoff

There I was, so many years later, standing in my dressing room with an anchorwoman thanking me for paving the way, for fighting for and getting equal pay for equal work.

I wish I could say I had stood up for all women in television—that would make for a better story of heroism. But the truth is, I just refused to be underpaid, and it was one of the toughest things I've ever done.

Her words in that moment made me reflect back over my career path and all I endured, including the demands and pressures I had faced starting out as a young journalist.

Especially if you are a young woman reading this book, I want you to write your own story in the workplace, to confidently communicate who you are and your value and worth. Stop doubting what you bring to the table. Sharpen your skills, so you'll have the tools, the armor, you need to succeed.

You must fight for the jobs and the salary that people say are out of reach. Fight for experiences and exposure in the workplace that have been closed to you.

At some point in your career, you've got to dive into the deep end and go for broke. Studies show that men typically ask for raises and women typically don't. Things will only get better when we start speaking up and bridge the wage gap.

Be careful not to lie or play hardball if you don't have the stomach for it. In case you're wondering, when faced with an ultimatum that day, my answer would have been no. I was no longer going to accept being underpaid for what I offered. With God's assurances, I was prepared to move on, if they refused to give me the salary I deserved.

My story might sound heroic, but I'm just a woman who knew her worth and pushed to be paid accordingly. A woman who discovered that God wants to prosper you, not to harm you, and give you hope and a future. Why was that discovery so agonizing? I believe He needed to teach me patience and endurance. To draw me closer to Him by reading the Word. I needed to learn to fight the thoughts of the enemy and believe God and His faithfulness, that He will do what He says He's going to do. He will do that for you, too, no matter your money struggles. I hope my story resonates with women who are afraid of demanding to be paid what they'd earned. Gender inequality in the workplace must change.

The ink was barely dry on my new deal when I realized what I had accomplished with God's help and I experienced a feeling I couldn't re-create in a thousand lifetimes. It was nearly an out-of-body experience to have held my ground and won. A girl from nowhere—part of the forgotten people, a girl who grew up in the bottom financial 99 percent of this country, had skyrocketed to become one of the top earners in her career.

*Chapter 17: My True Worth*

# Know Your Worth

Things have changed a lot for women since I first entered the workforce in the mid-1980s.

There are a lot more women in the workforce now. You might think that would make advocating for your worth easier, but pay inequality still exists, and we haven't moved the numbers much.

I believe it's even tougher today for women as companies continue to scale back and find ways to streamline and do more for less.

Women are entering male-dominated fields in greater numbers. In some fields, they actually prefer to hire women so they can pay them less. My husband, a former IT guy, says that women were always started at a lower salary in his field.

Life and work pushes us around at times. Some of us fight, and some give up. Some people really wanted to win, but the fear of losing forced them to back down. It can be excruciating to sit in front of multiple managers and have to prove what you bring to the table. They can team up and play games with your head. One may tear down your abilities, while the other builds you up again with flattery.

Your bravery can come off as arrogant if you're too forceful. It's not for everyone, hence the reason we have agents in television.

Young women especially still face a myriad of challenges in the corporate world. All the millennials I interviewed agreed that they are often stereotyped—branded as entitled. They say older colleagues tend to challenge their authority in leadership roles. They can get saddled with a heavier workload. Lowball salary offers seem to be the norm. Gender and age biases result in a lack of promotions, and their qualifications aren't taken into account. Black women in particular say that many times they feel marginalized and deal with microaggression.

Earlier in my career, a former news director rose from his desk and closed the space between us with heavy breathing and a searing, intimidating look after I rejected a contract offer. The hairs on my arms raised, an indication of my fear.

He was silent for a few moments, not uttering a word, just inching closer toward me as I sat still in my chair, trying desperately not to blink or twitch. He drew so close he could probably have sniffed my perfume.

Imagine coming face-to-face with a hungry grizzly bear with no way of escaping. It's just you and him—and he's sizing you up, waiting for you to make a move.

This man's negotiating style was a scare tactic unlike that of anyone I'd ever encountered in my thirty-year career. I doubt that tactic would ever be used on a man.

Trust me, the fear of not having a job can be daunting, but getting what you deserve requires reaching into your

## Chapter 17: My True Worth

reserves for strength. It's the courage God gives all of us.

Stop settling for less, believing you don't deserve more.

Expand your boundaries, and don't limit your knowledge to just your job. Listen to podcasts, take online courses—many are free. Get around and talk to people in the office who are doing different jobs—maybe one you aspire to have. Ask questions. It's been my experience that workers who are "winning" love to share how they did it.

Detectives solve crimes because they ask the right questions. You have to become a sleuth on the job. Know your industry, the history, the numbers, the salaries of others—some will give you a ballpark of where you should be.

Remember, a salary boost isn't the only way you can achieve your worth. Perks can sometimes be more important than a raise—more vacation time, a flexible schedule if you've got kids, the opportunity to learn a new skill, to travel, to work under a particular person as an apprentice.

We cannot let gender bias go unchallenged.

Finally, after my raise, I could buy Mom a home in a safer neighborhood. I would continue to help my friend who lived in a poorer school district send her two kids to a private school. I could put away money for my niece's college education. I gave a large donation to my church, supported several charities I'm passionate about, and shared with family members who needed help. God already knew the generosity in my heart.

I could have taken my huge bump in salary and invested in a bunch of material things—spending sprees, luxury cars, and unnecessary "stuff," but instead I started preparing for the financial freedom I dreamed of having, investing heavily in my future and things that mattered. I started thinking about what tomorrow might look like, on the day when I leave my career behind. I shored up my emergency fund. Then I socked away more money in my 401(k), in stocks and bonds, and in other retirement investments with the help of a great financial advisor. Be careful when seeking out a money planner. Do your homework and ask family and colleagues for recommendations.

Through that whole experience, I learned that the Lord was just waiting for me to trust Him. He needed me to be patient, manage my frustrations and anger, and continue to be obedient. When I carried around a spirit of doubt, I kept saying, "I think God is going to bless me. I hope He does, but what if He doesn't?" That is not faith.

> *Faith is being sure about what we hope for,*
> *being convinced about things we do not see.*
> **—Hebrews 11:1** EHV

This is my favorite verse in Scripture. We can't always see the blessings God is about to bestow upon us, but through faith, we believe it's coming.

*Chapter 17: My True Worth*

# EPILOGUE

As you've learned from my financial journey, attaining wealth is not only about hoping, wishing, and praying. It is about doing.

Genesis 2:15 tells us that "the Lord God placed the man in the Garden of Eden as its gardener, to tend and care for it" (TLB).

God immediately gave Adam a job to do—to cultivate and maintain His garden.

I believe He wants the same from us—to work and carefully watch over our financial favors. To renew our minds through prayer and search for different ways to pull ourselves out of any financial rut. To become good stewards by nurturing and growing our blessings and creating new things from the skills and tools He's given us.

Throughout my childhood, I didn't recognize my God-given skills. I was the kid who sat in the back row of the class, afraid the teacher would call on me.

I knew the right answers, but being extremely shy, I didn't want to be called on.

I walked in the shadow of my popular older sisters, until I grew up and realized I had something to offer, that I deserved to be given a seat at the table. I have never sat on the back row since.

My life began to change when I started to work on having a genuine and growing relationship with God—and becoming unafraid of what society thinks. You'll know when you're comfortable in your own skin because it will become clear you are not your money, your house, your car, or the material things you own.

I'm older, wiser, and stronger now. I never doubt God and His purpose in my life. He already knew the seeds I'd plant, how I'd maintain them, and how little or much they would grow to serve me and His people.

Second Corinthians 6:6 (NIV) warns against the trap of desiring wealth:

> *Whoever sows sparingly will also reap sparingly, and whoever sows generously will also reap generously.'*

God knows the economic harvest you're waiting on. He might be waiting to see if you'll do the work, using the skills and the talent He's provided you with. He knows your heart and whether He can trust you with financial gains.

> *If you want to know what God wants you to do, ask him, and he will gladly tell you, for he is always ready to give a bountiful supply of wisdom to all who ask him; he will not resent it.*
>
> —**James 1:5** TLB

Each day I work to live up to God's expectations, not

## Chapter 17: My True Worth

those of man. I know *who* I am and *whose* I am.

> *I know what it is to be in need, and I know what it is to have plenty. I have learned the secret of being content in any and every situation, whether well fed or hungry, whether living in plenty or in want.*
>
> **—Philippians 4:12** NIV

This scripture sums up the life I live.

Now you know the path I took that led to God's purpose for my life. His plan to prosper me and give me hope and a better future was not just for me. It was to serve His people.

My hope is that you will take some lessons from my journey that will set you on a new road to financial independence.

Living a life of purpose has afforded me the opportunity to support and share my testimony with young people, with women, and with any others who will listen.

No matter what your walk is in life, I hope you will feel a connection to my story and that it motivates you to reimagine your financial future. I hope you'll act and change your money attitude—allow yourself to be enough.

Saving is a mindset that has little to do with income levels. There are many high-income families who are poor on paper; they cannot afford their lifestyles, nor do they have any savings to fall back on. On the other hand, there are many low-income families who are financially sound. It is all about your priorities.

I sometimes have flashbacks of lessons in the Bible by which I've lived. I think of the passage that states, "Where there is no vision, the people perish" (Proverbs 29:18 KJV).

Envisioning what you want your life to look like and how you'll get there is critical.

Start now.

I've watched motivated people move; they act. People who are interested in doing better don't put off what they can do today, leaving it for tomorrow. People who have a budget, a plan, seek knowledge and advice.

And then there are those who are thinking about coming up with a plan; they don't own a calendar, and they never get around to it.

Challenge your complacency and determine why you're stuck.

Even if you've been throwing away good money, living above your means, or trying to adhere to societal pressures, I want the lessons in this book to show you a path forward when you're willing to adopt new money habits.

God can rain down financial favor in your life, replenish your cupboards, and pour out a blessing that you may not have room enough to receive (see Mal. 3:10). But you have to do the work.

*Chapter 17: My True Worth*

I am now at the age that every day is precious. I have lived more years than I have left on this earth, and I plan to continue to enjoy life to the fullest through my family and through writing, travel, and service.

> *Tell them to use their money to do good. They should be rich in good works, and generous to those in need, always being ready to share with others.*
> **—1 Timothy 6:18–19** NLT

By doing this they will be storing up their treasure as a good foundation for the future so that they may experience true life.

I do not have the audacity to try to tell you how you should give back. We all do things differently in our time and in a way that suits us. But I am a testament that you will gain favor from God when you understand why He chose to use you.

As a child, I couldn't see that being a ***poor girl*** would be the gift of my story. Now, as an adult, financial freedom is a security blanket that frees me up to do real work—God's work. And that's what living a ***rich life*** means to me.

# ACKNOWLEDGMENTS

I thank God for the talented people He brought into my life to see this book to fruition:

Christy Phillippe, my editor. Your skilled editing helped provide the pacing, cohesiveness, and fine-tuning my manuscript lacked.

Keely Boeving, an agent who believed in my project. Your input, skill, and guidance exceeded my expectations.

My friend Kelly Banks, you continue to be my rock when it comes to any writing roadblocks I face. You are always there with wise counsel. "Thank you" just never seems like enough.

Words cannot express my appreciation for my constant supporter and sister Melissa Robinson, who will tell me lovingly and sternly how she feels about the book. You are truly a godsend.

My sister Varnessa Robinson was short in her critiques, but on point when it came to needed changes.

My sister-in-law, Ramona Tyler, your eagerness to help in any way possible is so appreciated. Thanks for your internet searches and crucial feedback.

Thank you to the many friends and beta readers for going deeper and reading my book word for word and pointing out suggestions for younger readers who might be starved for wisdom.

My loving husband, Rodney, is still my biggest cheerleader and still reading my manuscript in between checking his sports news and scores to give me feedback.

To my many social media friends who always share my work, you are a godsend. I thank you for your support and kindness.

# ABOUT ROMONA

**Romona Robinson** is an eight-time Emmy Award–winning journalist, with thirty years of public speaking experience. She is a national award–winning author of *A Dirt Road to Somewhere*, *Your Voice Is Your Power*, and now, *Poor Girl, Rich Life*.

She is the founder of Romona's Kids, an Emmy-nominated television program–turned–institution in Cleveland, begun in 1990 to empower and encourage youth to find their path in life.

Romona is a television trailblazer, having become the first black female to anchor an evening broadcast in Cleveland. She was also the first woman to solo-anchor an evening newscast in the city. She is one of the most well-respected and admired journalists in northeast Ohio, having earned the trust of viewers for her integrity and unbiased reporting.

As a journalist, Romona has traveled the country, covering numerous presidents and world leaders, including Nelson Mandela and the late Ronald Reagan. In 2011, she garnered a rare exclusive interview with President Barack Obama. Along with her colleagues at station WOIO-TV 19, where she served as primary anchor, Romona won the coveted Edward R. Murrow Award in 2014.

She was inducted into the Press Club of Cleveland's Journalism Hall of Fame in 2016 and had the honor of receiving EWAW's Alpha Woman Award in 2017, which is given to women who exemplify strength in their field and use it to empower other women.

For twenty years, Romona served as the honorary chair of the Komen Race for the Cure, helping to bring awareness and hope to countless women enduring breast cancer. Romona's tireless work with children and her dedication to diversity issues have earned her such prestigious awards as the YWCA's Women of Achievement Award and The Diversity in Media Award.

Romona is also recognized for her powerful, dynamic messages as a motivational speaker.

Romona earned a bachelor of science degree in broadcast journalism from Lincoln University in Jefferson City, Missouri. Now Romona is frequently called upon to speak to women and children who need empowering messages of faith, hope, determination, and perseverance. She has traveled the state of Ohio and other parts of the nation, attending events from corporate affairs to meetings of various women's organizations. She firmly believes we all have something to offer to the world—we just have to allow God to lead us.

## STAY CONNECTED WITH ROMONA

🌐 romonarobinson.com

📘 @Romona's Room

📘 @Romona Robinson

📷 @RomonaRobinson

🐦 @romonarobinson

in Romona Robinson

**If you enjoyed my book,
an Amazon review would be greatly appreciated.**

Part of the proceeds of this book will be donated to organizations that serve the needs of children.

### Contact Romona Robinson for speaking requests:

Website: romonarobinson.com

Telephone: 800-296-8232